The Myth *of* Christian America

What You Need to Know

About the Separation

Of Church and State

D1073325

Mark Weldon Whitten

SMYTH&HELWYS
PUBLISHING, INCORPORATED   MACON, GEORGIA

Smyth & Helwys Publishing, Inc.
6316 Peake Road
Macon, Georgia 31210-3960
1-800-747-3016
© 1999 by Smyth & Helwys Publishing
All rights reserved.
Printed in the United States of America.

Mark Weldon Whitten

The paper used in this publication meets the minimum
requirements of American National Standard for Information
Sciences—Permanence of Paper for Printed Library Materials.
ANSI Z39.48–1984 (alk. paper)

Library of Congress Cataloging-in-Publication Data

Whitten, Mark Weldon.
    The myth of "Christian America":
    what you need to know about the separation of church and state
    p.   cm.
    Includes bibliographical references.
    1. Church and state—United States.
    2. Freedom of religion—United States.
    I. Title.
    BR516.W448   1999
    322'.1'0973—dc21   99-14806
                                                   CIP
ISBN 1-57312-287-4

Contents

The late Brooks Hays, quintessential Baptist, loved to say, "We are all conservative sometimes and liberal sometimes. We're like my old dog Fergus here who is a conservative when he buries a bone, but liberal when he chases a rabbit."

Mark Weldon Whitten captures the marvelous ambiguities attendant upon finding a proper relationship between church and state. His work makes a useful contribution to this pursuit.

We Americans tend to politicize and polarize everything. All ideas and initiatives are liberal or conservative, good or bad, right or wrong. This damned dualism infects all our belief and behavior. (That's a theological assessment.) Yet the first sixteen words of the Bill of Rights offer parallel challenges.

Whitten does a useful service in graphically setting out the tension between absolute separation of church and state and an unlimited free exercise of religion. He makes the case for creative and constructive tension between these complimentary concepts. With an eloquent economy of words he describes an in-between strategy. He contends for a both/and, not an either/or approach.

If Jefferson's "wall of separation" is less than the ideal metaphor to describe the constitutional distance between church and state, perhaps a "wall with many doors" suggested by Stephen Carter makes sense. Or maybe Martin Marty is right: a "zone" may describe the present space between these institutions. Whitten and I hope that at least a strand of "barbed wire" will keep either church or state from holding the other in a bearhug.

Whitten offers an appropriate word about the inevitable ambiguity, the necessity of creative tension between no establishment of religion and the free exercise thereof, a welcome addition to the literature.

—*James M. Dunn*

"It takes two to speak the truth—one to speak, and another to hear."

—*Henry David Thoreau*

"He who begins by loving 'Christianity' better than Truth will proceed by loving his own sect or church better than Christianity, and end in loving himself better than all."

—*Samuel Taylor Coleridge*

"Congress shall make no law respecting an establishment of religion, or prohibiting the free exercise thereof . . ."

—*First Amendment*
U.S. Constitution

The Myth of the Myth of Church-State Separation

This book is designed to communicate the constitutional philosophy and principle of church-state separation to pastors, laypersons, and anyone who is not conversant with the discipline of church-state studies. The intent is to counter the mythology and misinformation that is widely being perpetrated among conservative Christians today concerning the purposes of the Founding Fathers in their establishment of the United States of America by the Declaration of Independence in 1776 and in the rights of the nation outlined in the Constitution of 1787.

Many conservative Christians advocate that our Founding Fathers intended to establish the United States as a "Christian" nation and based their efforts directly for sake of the Christian religion. This misinformation also contends that "Christian" denominations merit special privileges and protection from the state that are not the rights of other religions and therefore, that church-state separation is a "myth"—a falsehood or a lie.

This mythological view of the origins and nature of our nation is grounded in and supportive of an "establishment mentality" and agenda on the part of fundamentalist Christians who will be referred to in the following essays as the Religious Right. Speaking of some contemporary Baptists whose forebears had such a significant role in instituting religious liberty and church-state separation in our nation, Glenn Hinson wrote,

> Majority status has not only dampened concern [for religious liberty], it has tended to create an *establishment mentality*, one that seeks special favors for the majority. . . . In subtle ways, despite the

guarantees of the Constitution, Protestants sometimes have taken advantage of their majority in the United States to assure dominance in public life.[1]

It is indeed ironic that evangelical Protestants who sought free exercise and no establishment of religion when they were minorities subsequently seek to preserve or regain governmental accommodation, preference, privilege, and quasi-establishment for their particular brand of religion. In the words of Hinson, "As they have become the religious majority, they have sought accommodation—quasi-establishment—and have become considerably less sympathetic to the free exercise rights of minorities."[2] It is in opposition to this establishment mentality and agenda that these essays are presented.

The apostles of a Christian America contend that the philosophy and principle of church-state separation is a myth or lie of recent provenance. The essays in this book succinctly demonstrate that it is the denial of church-state separation, properly understood, that constitutes error and myth-making. They set forth what Americans need to know about proper relations between religion, Christian or otherwise, and government in our nation. They affirm, develop, and defend a number of significant theses with regards to religious liberty and church-state separation. Following are brief introductions to each essay:

Chapter 1

The religion clauses of the First Amendment are the explicit constitutional guarantee of religious liberty. Narrow interpretation of the Free Exercise and Non-establishment clauses, however, is being advocated by opponents of church-state separation. Some seek to justify accommodation and non-preferential aid to Christian denominations that would not be conferred upon non-Christian religions. Non-Christian religions would not benefit from constitutional protection of their religious liberty. Such a narrow interpretation of the religion clauses is not consistent with the history, text, and ideals of the Constitution nor with the ideals of authentic Christianity.

Chapter 2

The Founding Fathers did not intend to establish the United States of America as a Christian nation. In fact, the history surrounding the Constitutional Convention of 1787, the resulting Constitutional text, its ratification, the adoption of the First Amendment by the First Congress, and subsequent practice by presidents, particularly Thomas Jefferson and James Madison, demonstrate that church-state separation was the mainstream intent and practice.

Chapter 3

Church-state separation is the ideal that should be pursued in often-thorny questions of the proper relations between religion and government. However, it cannot and should not be instituted in an absolute or maximally strict manner. Metaphors such as Jefferson's "wall of separation" can be both helpful and misleading. It is not easy to select a better metaphor than Jefferson's for church-state separation. Jefferson's wall of separation must be recognized for what it is—a metaphor for an ideal, and not an agenda or a blueprint for an absolutely attainable reality and relationship.

Chapter 4

Far from being a myth or a lie, church-state separation is a constitutional principle and philosophy that is enshrined within the First Amendment, particularly within the non-establishment clause. The assertion that the United States of America was founded as a "Christian nation" is itself a myth, an historically false and politically pernicious assertion that endangers religious liberty.

Chapter 5

The proceedings of the Constitutional Convention of 1787 were a demonstration and example of church-state separation. They evidence the falsity of the assertion that the Founding Fathers sought to create a Christian America. The worldview myth of Christian America produces an ideology that leads some members of the Religious Right to misinterpret the historical evidence and to misconstrue the foundations and nature of our nation and its republican institutions.

Chapter 6

First Amendment protection of religious liberty is properly applied or extended to all religions and to all religious or non-religious persons, not just to the Christian religion and to Christians. This is clearly recognized when the Constitution is interpreted with careful attention to its textual wording and to the Declaration of Independence as interpretive background and guide.

Chapter 7

There is a logical tension and often a practical conflict between the Free Exercise and Non-Establishment clauses of the First Amendment. Denial of such tension and conflicts is expressive of ideological and absolutist strategies of either absolute/strict separationism or absolute/maximal accommodationism. Recognition of the tension requires a dialectical understanding of the relation between the two religion clauses and a more nuanced understanding of church-state separation.

Chapter 8

There are two strategies one may follow in the pursuit of religious liberty and application of First Amendment protection of religious liberty. One may pursue a separationist strategy that guards against establishments of religion, or one may pursue an accommodationist strategy that promotes free exercise of religion. If either strategy is pursued in an absolute manner, religious liberty will suffer. Both strategies must be advocated, opposed to one another, and balanced with one another.

Chapter 9

Political differences are rooted in different mindsets with different attitudes towards social change: conservative preservationism and liberal progressivism. Each mindset provokes political strategies that potentially result in both benefits and harms to society. Conservatives and liberals are needed in the pursuit of the common good of society, and both accommodationists and separationists are needed to pursue and to preserve the common good of religious liberty.

This book makes available on the popular level the benefit of the investigations of competent, reputable scholars regarding the validity and necessity of the doctrine of church-state separation. Average laypersons have little time, access to resources, or encouragement to consult scholarly works on the matter of religious liberty. As a result, they often fall prey to the slipshod and superficial teachings of ideologues and demagogues spoken from pulpits in our churches or written in texts found in our local Christian bookstores.

The concern of this book is not merely intellectual in character. While it examines errors of historical or political-scientific reasoning, its concern is pastoral in nature. Errors in matters of the relation of church and state bring potential harm to the church's witness to truth and to Christ in American society. The Church of Jesus Christ is not likely to be recognized as an exponent of spiritual liberty if it makes itself an opponent of political liberty!

Also contained within the following pages are my original arguments. These arguments are often blunt and polemical in presentation, but they are not intended to discount or discredit the Christian character of those who disagree with my conclusions or with the philosophy of church-state separation. Their energetic espousal are, however, intended to discredit what I feel to be dangerously un-Christian and un-American ideas and teachings on the relation of religion and government in our nation. Only God can judge the heart, but responsible Christians and Americans are required by truth and conscience to judge, to expose, and to oppose erroneous and subversive teachings and ideologies.

This book is organized so as to be readily accessible to study groups on religious liberty. Each chapter is a self-contained essay and can be used without necessary reference to previous chapters. There is, therefore, some slight duplication of material between chapters to enable each chapter and its subject matter to stand alone.

It is my desire that this book provide a clear, competent, properly-nuanced exposition and defense of church-state separation for the support of religious liberty at all levels of our polity and for all citizens of our nation. I am grateful to those who have instructed me in matters of religious liberty, most of them known to myself only through their research and writings, and who have informed my views concerning church-state separation. I am especially grateful to my Baptist forebears who paid a much higher price than I ever expect to pay to establish and defend religious liberty and church-state separation in our nation. This book is offered as a small companion and addition to their work.

Special thanks go to those persons who have encouraged me in the pursuit of this writing project: Jim Bankston, Paul Basden, Joe Blair, David Capes, Francette Carnahan, Charlotte and Don Coffelt, Krishna Cook, Darlene Corbitt, David Currie, Derek Davis, Curtis Freeman, Gary Furr, James Leo Garrett, Jack Harwell, E. Glenn Hinson, Fisher Humphreys, Olin Joynton, Joe Phelps, Bruce Prescott, Walter Shurden, Camille Swart, Bob Tucker, and Bill Turner. I especially want to thank James Dunn for his foreword and my editor, Jackie Riley, for her patience and invaluable assistance with this, my first book.

This book is dedicated to my mother and father, Vivian and Weldon Whitten, in appreciation for their gifts of life, nurture, education, and freedom to be myself. I hope to pass on the same to their grandsons, John Weldon Whitten II and Hunt Maddox Whitten.

Notes

[1]E. Glenn Hinson, *Religious Liberty: The Christian Roots of Our Fundamental Freedoms* (Louisville KY: Glad River Publications, 1991) 133.

[2]Warren A. Nord, *Religion and American Education: Rethinking a National Dilemma* (Chapel Hill NC: University of North Carolina Press, 1995) 122.

Chapter 1

Religious Liberty for Me, But Not for Thee?

The religion clauses of the First Amendment to the United States Constitution guarantee religious liberty to all citizens of the nation. Separation of church and state has been the interpretive philosophy by which the Supreme Court has understood the "Free Exercise" and "non-establishment" clauses of the First Amendment. Justice Hugo Black declared in *Everson vs. Board of Education* (1947): "Neither a state nor the federal government can set up a church. Neither can pass laws which aid one religion, aid all religions, or prefer one religion over another." Justice William O. Douglas wrote in *Zorach vs. Clauson* (1952):

> There cannot be the slightest doubt that the First Amendment reflects the philosophy that church and state should be separated. And so far as interference with the "free exercise" of religion and an "establishment" of religion are concerned, the separation must be complete and unequivocal.

There are a number of decisive evidences that support the Supreme Court's separationist philosophy, even though the words "separation of church and state" are not contained in the text of the Constitution.[1] The chief consideration, of course, is the text of the Constitution. Justice Wiley Rutledge acutely recognized in *Everson vs. Board of Education*:

> The Amendment's purpose was not to strike merely at the official establishment of a single sect, creed, or religion . . . The object was broader than separating church and state in the narrow sense. . . .

"Religion" appears only once in the Amendment. But the word governs two prohibitions, and it governs them alike. It does not have two meanings, one narrow to forbid an "establishment" and another, much broader, for securing the "free exercise thereof.". . . Congress and now the states are as broadly restricted concerning the one as they are the other.

The Religious Right[2] advocates of a "Christian America" reject the constitutional philosophy of church-state separation and deny that the First Amendment prohibits nonpreferential aid to religion in general (actually, "Christianity"—as they practice and define it). They affirm that government support of religion is constitutionally permissible as long as one religion (one denomination of Christianity) is not preferentially supported over others.

The logic of a nonpreferentialist interpretation of the First Amendment entails radical and disturbing consequences for the protection of the religious liberty of all citizens of our nation. Rejection of church-state separation in favor of a nonpreferentialist philosophy, combined with a narrow meaning of "religion" applied to the dual prohibitions of the religion clauses of the First Amendment, permits a denial of constitutional protection of religious liberty to all non-Christian religions and citizens.

David Barton, a chief propagandist for the notion of America as a Christian nation and an opponent of church-state separation, seeks to interpret the religion clauses of the First Amendment according to "original intent" and "strict construction" of the Constitutional text. To arrive at the [sic] original intent of these clauses and their terminology, he appeals to the state constitutions of the constitutional era.

The states themselves did not allow one denomination of Christianity to be the official denomination . . . Even when the state constitutions stated that their citizens had a right to worship God according to their conscience, a statement immediately followed stipulating that it be within Christian standards. In other words, as long as someone was pursuing some form of orthodox Christianity, he was protected in his freedom of worship and conscience. The constitutions did not guarantee that freedom outside of traditional Christianity.[3]

Barton thus holds to a narrow meaning of religion for both the non-establishment and Free Exercise clauses. He maintains that the government cannot establish or prefer a particular Christian church or denomination *or* prohibit the free exercise of the same.

But if such a narrow construal of religion and the protection of religious liberty by the First Amendment is accepted, the Constitution does not protect the religious liberty of persons and religions that are not Christian. David Barton specifically denies that First Amendment protection of religious liberty is properly extended to atheism and secular humanism by functional interpretations of religion. He also evidently asserts that other non-Christian religious groups are not included within constitutional guarantees of free exercise and non-establishment.

In his first book, *The Myth of Separation*, Barton denied that atheism, secular humanism, or "other groups" that have been granted the status of "religion" by the Supreme Court actually qualify for protection under the First Amendment religous liberty provisions.[4] In his more recent work, *Original Intent*, he holds that the First Amendment was enacted for a very specific and narrow purpose—to disallow federal establishment of any particular Christian denomination. He denies that the First Amendment was intended or understood to promote or to protect religious pluralism.[5]

Harold O. J. Brown, an evangelical Christian professor of theology, similarly advocated,

> The state should give the status of church only to those bodies which satisfy a scholarly, descriptive definition of orthodoxy. This requirement will be considered legislating "respecting an establishment of religion" and is unconstitutional according to the current interpretation of the First Amendment. But we need not view it that way. . . . When the First Amendment was adopted, there was a general consensus among Americans as to what constituted a Christian church. . . . In a Christian America it will be necessary to distinguish between churches on the one hand and other religious bodies, groups, and organizations on the other.[6]

For advocates of a Christian America such as Barton and Brown, only Christian churches and denominations would benefit from full and equal First Amendment protection of religious liberty!

But what constitutes a "Christian" church or denomination? A Christian religious group extant in the 1780s and recognized to be such by the Founding Fathers and their original intent? If not, what would be the contemporary criteria for a Christian church or denomination? Who would decide upon and apply the criteria? The legislatures and courts influenced by the Religious Right?

What about a professedly Christian church or denomination—for example, the Church of Jesus Christ of Latter Day Saints or Churches of Christ, Scientist (Christian Science)—that failed to meet the criteria and to be judged Christian? What about liberal Christian churches who are viewed as heretical by fundamentalist Christianity? Even the religious liberty of professed Christian churches might be threatened by a narrow, nonpreferentialist interpretation of the First Amendment.

David Barton's books, from which the preceding arguments and quotes are taken, are often not reliable in their appeals to evidence and arguments. But to many in the Religious Right, David Barton is something of a guru on constitutional matters, which makes the logic and espousal of his views more disturbing and possibly dangerous to religious liberty. One will do well in these matters to heed the warning of the "Father of the U.S. Constitution," James Madison:

> Who does not see that the same authority which can establish Christianity, in exclusion of all other religions, may establish with the same ease any particular sect of Christians, in exclusion of all other sects? That the same authority which can force a citizen to contribute three pence only of his property for the support of any one establishment, may force him to conform to any other establishment in all cases whatsoever?[7]

Note: the Christian America that would result from the implementation of a narrow, nonpreferentialist, anti-church/state separationist construal of the First Amendment guarantees of free exercise and non-establishment would result in a nation that is neither authentically Christian nor American. Indeed it would be a different America than that envisioned by the saints and patriots who gave their lives for a nation that guarantees "liberty and justice *for all*." Quite honestly, such a view is profoundly and dangerously subversive. Richard Taylor was right on target when he wrote,

A political conservative, within the framework of United States politics, tries to conserve something quite specific—namely, the values embedded in the Constitution. . . . If anyone were to try to replace the Constitution by, say, the Koran, then no one would doubt that this would be an act of subversion. . . . Similarly, for anyone to subordinate the principles embodied in the Constitution to those of the Bible, or to those of one of the various churches or creeds claiming scripture as its source, is political subversion.[8]

Our American ideals of liberty and equality for all—as enshrined in our Pledge of Allegiance, Declaration of Independence, and Constitution—and authentic Christianity—a religion of Christlike love, humility, and freedom—can never countenance a sectarian hijacking of the Constitution that promotes religious liberty for me, but not for thee.

How is it that we have come so far as a nation and as Christian citizens that such a dangerous and intellectually flawed rejection of church-state separation and religious liberty for all Americans can be seriously advocated and accepted? Misunderstanding of the origins and purposes of contemporary separationist interpretation of the religion clauses of the First Amendment at least partly accounts for the present situation.

It is rightly recognized that the First Amendment protection of religious liberty was originally applied only to actions of the federal government, specifically the United States Congress,[9] although presidents such as Thomas Jefferson and James Madison also considered themselves bound by the free exercise and non-establishment prohibitions. It was not until *Cantwell vs. Connecticut* (1940) that the Supreme Court decreed that the Free Exercise Clause applied to the states. In the 1947 decision *Everson vs. Board of Education*, both the Free Exercise and Non-Establishment Clauses were "incorporated" and applied to the states.

The application of the First Amendment to state actions was entirely appropriate given the falsity of the compact theory of the national union,[10] the adoption of the Fourteenth Amendment to the Constitution in 1868,[11] and the foundational and guiding character of the Declaration of Independence and the natural rights of "life, liberty, and the pursuit of happiness" for Constitutional interpretation.[12] Furthermore, rather than the *Everson* decision being viewed as the onslaught of a Supreme Court's anti-God, anti-religion judicial activism (as it is often presented today within the Religious Right), evangelical Christians of the day were concerned that separation of church and state was, in fact, being compromised by the decision.

In his 1948 publication, *Separate Church and State Now!* (1948), J. M. Dawson gave contemporary testimony to the alarm with which the Court's decision was viewed by evangelical Christians. They feared that church-state separation and religious liberty were being compromised and threatened by a a socially aggressive American Catholicism that had been historically opposed to religious liberty and its necessary corollary of church-state separation.[13] According to Dawson,

> In the course of time, questions have arisen which have called for clarification of the principle of separation of church and state. Currently the matter is a subject of intense debate throughout the country. Not only does the discussion wax hot on theoretical grounds, but concrete cases involving the principle are presented for decision by the people in elections, members of legislatures in law-making, jurists in legal opinions, executives who administer the law, and by churchmen who advocate policies. It is highly important, if possible, therefore, that a satisfactory definition be generally accepted.[14]

An ambassador to the Vatican had been retained by President Harry Truman, a situation that many then (and now) consider to be a privilege of Roman Catholicism and a violation of religious liberty—specifically the Non-Establishment Clause—and church-state separation. The National Association of Evangelicals was one among many Protestant denominations and groups that opposed such an appointment. It warned in April 1947,

> This United States-Vatican relationship is already beginning to fan the flames of intolerance and bigotry and will inevitably result in the introduction of the religious issue into American politics.[15]

In 1948 an archbishop was appointed for Washington, D.C. At the local levels of American society, Catholics were pursuing more equitable social standing in actions that contradicted the *de facto* cultural and, in many places and instances, political establishment of

Protestantism. A chief battleground consisted of the public and Catholic parochial school systems. For instance, in the College Hill section of Cincinnati, Ohio, a Catholic majority took over a public school and ran it at public expense. The Council of Churches of Cincinnati declared,

> The people did not seem to have been greatly concerned about the inclusion of the parochial school in the public school system until the Roman Catholic majority began their frontal attack upon the whole public school system in apparent determination to control it for their own purposes.[16]

A more widespread point of contention involved efforts by Roman Catholics to obtain some financial relief from state governments from the burdens of maintaining their own parochial school systems. *Everson vs. Board of Education* was brought before the Supreme Court on 10 February 1947 to determine the constitutionality of a New Jersey law and local school board practice that allowed (Catholic) parents to be reimbursed by the state for expenses incurred in busing their children to school. (The constitutionality of the law was upheld at the same time that church-state separation was affirmed in the decision.) By 1948, eighteen states had passed legislation permitting financial support of sectarian religious schools in one form or another, and two bills were being considered in Congress that would permit the distribution of federal funds by the states to parochial schools.[17]

While the Everson decision espoused a separationist philosophy of First Amendment interpretation, it pronounced an accommodational decision that many saw as inconsistent with separationism and religious liberty, and the possible first instance of many more such violations. The decision of the five-justice majority was widely protested, and the dissent of the four justice minority widely affirmed throughout the nation.

> The five-to-four decision . . . to use the words of the Horace Mann League, "caused considerable discussion, many protests, and some anxiety upon the part of the general public as well as among educators." It is not too much to say that in general the newspaper press of the Nation condemned the decision of the Court's majority and accepted the opinion of the four dissenting justices.[18]

J. M. Dawson emphasized that, at least at its best, the protest against the Court's decision was not an expression of religious intolerance toward Catholicism:

> We non-Catholics who are engaged in this high endeavor must make it clear that we are not inspired by religious differences but by our common political convictions concerning the religious liberty of all faiths. . . . We repeat and emphasize that we do not suggest, much less advocate, an anti-Catholic campaign. . . . We affirm our complete devotion to the principle of equal rights for all religious faiths, and insist on absolute equity for the Catholics, with no semblance of persecution of them or imposition of any disabilities whatsoever. This aim is consistent with the best Protestant tradition in America.[19]

It was also at this time that the major Protestant denominations set up offices in Washington, D.C., to lobby for religious liberty and church-state concerns.[20] J. M. Dawson led the Baptist presence that was later to be named the Baptist Joint Committee on Public Affairs. Also during this time and within this historical and social context, the organization "Protestants and Other Americans United for the Separation of Church and State" (now "Americans United for Separation of Church and State") was organized.

The crusade for freedom of religion (or no religion) was extended to worldwide concern. Specifically, following World War II, there was an international concern for liberty and human rights, as expressed in the charter of the new United Nations. As an expression of the concern that all peoples of the world enjoy the blessings of religious liberty, the Seventh Baptist World Congress published a Manifesto in 1947 that declared this concern. The Manifesto also called upon Baptists to transform the fundamental principles of liberty contained therein into positive action and a "worldwide crusade for freedom."[21]

Thus, mid-century advocacy of church-state separation and subsequent separationist Supreme Court decisions must be viewed within the context of a widespread religious concern for the preservation of American principles of liberty, equality, and justice for all American citizens in their religious convictions and also a world-encompassing concern that such liberties be enjoyed by all peoples.

There is not a hint of animosity toward religion in the separationist efforts and philosophy of the Baptist advocate of religious liberty, J. M.

Dawson. Dawson promoted *full* religious liberty for *all* American citizens; the religion of no one was merely to be tolerated or relegated to second-class status. Quite picturesquely, he wrote:

> The struggle between weasel toleration granted by majorities and full religious liberty as sought by minorities is, therefore, of supreme moment; for the whole world must be convinced of the deplorable inferiority of the former as compared with the glorious principle of the latter.[22]

Nor were hostile intentions against religion or religious liberty behind the opinions of Baptist Supreme Court Justice Hugo Black, in deciding the *Everson* case.

It is within the context of a commitment to church-state separation as a necessary and constitutional means to religious liberty that modern jurisprudence of the First Amendment must be appreciated. Neither the Supreme Court nor advocates of church-state separation have purposed to deny religious liberty in their interpretations of the First Amendment. Church-state separationists are, however, properly recognized to oppose efforts on the part of religious majorities or powerful and militant minorities who seek to maintain or achieve privileged status or special benefits from government under the guise of "free exercise."

Interpretation of the First Amendment in terms of church-state separation is rightfully seen as a bulwark against any attempt by any group, Christian or otherwise, to deny religious liberty to any citizen or religion, seeking "religious liberty for me, but not for thee."

Discussion Questions

1. Do you believe that *all* American citizens should enjoy full and *equal* religious liberty? Why or why not?
2. Some Christian groups have recited the Pledge of Allegiance with the following conclusion: ". . . with liberty and justice *for all who believe*." What is your reaction toward this way of thinking?
3. Why would a member of a majority religion, for example, the Baptist J. M. Dawson, affirm church-state separation?
4. What is the difference between full and equal religious liberty and religious *toleration*?

Notes

[1]See chapter 2.

[2]"Religious Right" refers to those fundamentalist and conservative-evangelical Christians who are highly active politically and who have been politically mobilized in parachurch organizations such as the Christian Coalition. They are generally supportive of populist-conservative or right-wing political causes and the Republican Party. There are, of course, many fundamentalist and conservative Christians who are not so involved.

[3]David Barton, *The Myth of Separation: What Is the Correct Relationship Between Church and State?* (Aledo TX: Wallbuilder Press, 1992) 29.

[4]Ibid., 30.

[5]David Barton, *Original Intent: The Courts, the Constitution, and Religion* (Aledo TX: Wallbuilder Press, 1996) 31.

[6]Harold O. J. Brown, "The Christian America View," in *God and Politics: Four Views on the Reformation of Civil Government*, ed. Gary Scott Smith (Phillipsburg NY: Presbyterian and Reformed Publishing Co., 1987) 145-46.

[7]This quotation is taken from James Madison's "Memorial and Remonstrance." One might also take to heart the warning of Samuel Taylor Coleridge that "he who begins by loving Christianity better than Truth will proceed by loving his own sect or church better than Christianity, and end in loving himself better than all."

[8]Richard Taylor, *Reflective Wisdom: Richard Taylor on Issues That Matter*, ed. John Donnelly (Buffalo NY: Prometheus Books, 1989) 123-24.

[9]*Barron vs. Baltimore* (1834) specifically declared that the Bill of Rights did not apply to the states.

[10]The compact theory of national union holds that the states created the federal union, that the states are the foundational units of our national polity, and that the states are not subject to constitutional restrictions originally applied only to the national government. It follows that the states may either protect or reject fundamental human rights according to the texts of their state constitutions or the whims of their legislative majorities. This was the Confederate view of national union espoused by secessionist John C. Calhoun. It was a view opposed by Abraham Lincoln who held that the national union began as an act of the American people when they declared their independence from Britain and established themselves as a people, not as multiple separate and independent sovereign states. Lincoln's views were grounded in the constitutional views of luminaries such as James Madison, Alexander Hamilton, John Marshall, Joseph Story, James Wilson, and a host of others. It is truly amazing that advocates of "states rights" have almost invariably made their claims for exemption from the First Amendment and other constitutional guarantees of human rights in favor of some restriction upon the liber-

ties of minorities—in race, political views, or religion. It is shocking that they do so in contradiction to the spirit and doctrines of the eminent American forefathers previously mentioned. It is dishonest that they do so with the claim that their view was "the original understanding" of the national union. And it is appalling that they do so in the name of Christianity!

[11]The Fourteenth Amendment constitutionally altered the relation between the states and the federal government in significant ways. Its "privileges and immunities" and "due process" clauses are essential for understanding the propriety of Supreme Court "incorporation" of the First Amendment and application of First Amendment protection of rights to actions of the states.

[12]Briefly, interpretation of the United States Constitution must be informed by the principles of union of the American nation as stated in the Declaration of Independence and by the purposes designated in the constitution's Preamble. Any law or interpretation of the Constitution that violates the security of citizens' natural rights of "life, liberty, and the pursuit of happiness," for instance, is an unconstitutional law or an unsound interpretation.

[13]It is an anachronistic objection that concern by Protestants over Roman Catholicism's commitment to religious liberty in America was merely an expression of anti-Catholic bigotry. Vatican II and the fruition of the efforts of John Courtney Murray in reforming Catholicism's views on the relation of institutional government and religion in America lay yet in the future. While we live in different circumstances today, and while some concerns may have been overblown, official Roman Catholic pronouncements, historic church-state policies, and some contemporary actions did constitute cause for concern at that time.

[14]Joseph Martin Dawson, *Separate Church and State Now!* (New York: Richard R. Smith, 1948) 33.

[15]Ibid., 77.

[16]Ibid., 83-84.

[17]Ibid., 203.

[18]Ibid., 52.

[19]Ibid., 85-86.

[20]Ibid., 89.

[21]Ibid., 158.

[22]Ibid., 128.

Chapter 2

The Facts of
Church-State Separation

A popular, pious, and dangerously mistaken falsehood is being promoted among and by many Christian groups today: that the United
States of America was founded to be a "Christian nation." In the
Religious Right, for example, Rick Scarborough, a Baptist minister,
fantasizes:

> America has not been lucky; she has been blessed. She is the product
> of the determination of our forebears to forge a nation built upon
> biblical principles. As they labored to create a Christian nation, God
> looked with affection and favor upon their efforts and gave them
> supernatural guidance that enabled them to author foundational
> documents unlike any the world had ever seen before. The wisdom
> of our Declaration of Independence and Constitution can only be
> described as inspired. Truly the hand of God was driving the
> thoughts and decisions of those men.[1]

Those who promote the theory that America was founded as a
Christian nation therefore believe that separation of church and state
is a "lie" or a "myth" because the concept is not precisely stated in the
Constitution of the United States. David Barton, popular apologist for
this type of error, asserts:

> Most people are surprised when they find that the Constitution does
> not contain the words "separation of church and state." The com-
> mon perception is that those words are the heart of the First Amend-
> ment and are included in it. There is no "wall of separation" in the
> Constitution unless it is a wall intended by the Founding Fathers to

keep the government out of the church. The doctrine of separation of church and state is absurd; it has been repeated often; and people have believed it.[2]

How accurate are statements and judgments such as these? Is church-state separation an absurdity and a myth? Or is the denial of church-state separation as a constitutional philosophy and principle itself an absurdity—a travesty of the interpretation of the constitutional history and text that is being repeated often and unjustifiably believed by many?

While the Religious Right argues against the principle of separation of church and state because the actual words are not contained in the text of the Constitution, they affirm the concept of separation of powers—another phrase noticeably absent from the Constitution. Similarly, members of the Religious Right who reject church-state separation are predominantly Christian trinitarian theists, even though the term "Trinity" is not found in the Bible. Do they therefore wish to deny that trinitarian theology is a biblical doctrine?

The real issue is not whether the words "separation of church and state" are found in the Constitution; the real issue is whether or not the principle is a constitutional assumption, and what this philosophy actually entails in practice. The following eight decisive evidences demonstrate that church-state separation is a constitutional assumption and principle.

(1) No theological or biblical arguments and no prayers for divine guidance or approval were offered during the Constitutional Convention of 1787, contrary to what contemporary myth-makers such as David Barton have irresponsibly asserted. In fact, delegate Gouverneur Morris declared on the floor of the Convention on July 2, days after an ill-fated motion by Benjamin Franklin to introduce public prayers into the Convention proceedings: "Reason tells us we are but men, and we are not to expect any particular interference of Heaven in our favor."[3]

(2) The text of the Constitution makes no appeals to religious authorities, rationales, or purposes. The Constitution is a "Godless document," a fact that was immediately evident to evangelical Christians of the constitutional era. Timothy Dwight, evangelical president of Yale University declared:

The nation has offended Providence. We formed our constitution without any acknowledgment of God; without any recognition of His mercies to us as a people, of his government or even of his existence. The [Constitutional] Convention, by which it was formed, never asked, even once, His direction, or His blessings, upon their labors. Thus we commenced our national existence under the present system without God.[4]

(3) Article VI., clause 3 of the Constitution—the only substantive mention of religion in the Constitution—prohibits any religious tests for holding political office. It was rightly recognized by most citizens at the time (and wrongly objected to by many) that this restriction allowed a member of any religion, or none at all, to serve in the federal government.

(4) The *Federalist Papers*—written by Alexander Hamilton, James Madison, and John Jay to "sell" the new Constitution to the American people—made no appeal to religious authorities, rationales, or purposes to legitimize the Constitution.

(5) Although Thomas Jefferson, author of the letter to Danbury Baptists that contains the phrase "wall of separation," was not a member of the Constitutional Convention, James Madison was. Madison was the most influential member of the Constitutional Convention and was the driving force behind the creation and adoption of the Bill of Rights. He was the architect of the First Amendment with its guarantees of free exercise and non-establishment of religion. As President, Madison practiced a strict separation of church and state. He wrote:

There remains . . . a strong bias toward the old error, that without some sort of alliance or coalition between Gov[ernmen]t & Religion, neither can be duly supported. Such indeed is the tendency to such a coalition, and such is its corrupting influence on both the parties, that the danger cannot be too carefully guarded ag[ains]t. . . . Every new & successful example therefore of a perfect separation between ecclesiastical and civil matters is of importance. And I have no doubt that every new example will succeed, as every past one has done, in shewing that religion & Gov[ernmen]t will both exist in greater purity, the less they are mixed together.[5]

(6) The debate in the First Congress on the wording of the First Amendment demonstrates that it was designed and understood to disallow not only particular and preferential aid to one Christian denomination over others, but also nonpreferential aid to religion in general. Wording that would have allowed nonpreferential aid to Christian denominations in general was carefully considered and rejected.[6] Douglas Laycock has concluded that such an interpretation of the Establishment Clause produced by the First Congress is inconsistent with the facts:

> Nonpreferentialism is one of the few issues the founders clearly considered and decided. Nonpreferentialism was the last compromise offered by the defenders of establishment, and the founding generation repeatedly rejected it.[7]

(7) The text of the First Amendment refutes the idea that it does not embody the principle of church-state separation. As Justice Wiley Rutledge incisively and decisively wrote in the Supreme Court decision *Zorach vs. Clauson* (1952),

> The amendment's purpose was not to strike merely at the official establishment of a single sect, creed, or religion . . . The object was broader than separation of church and state in the narrow sense . . . "Religion" appears only once in the amendment. But the word governs two prohibitions, and it governs them alike. It does not have two meanings, one narrow to forbid an "establishment" and another, much broader, for securing "the free exercise thereof." Congress and now the states are as broadly restricted concerning the one as they are the other.

Douglas Laycock has discerned well that the text of the First Amendment does not say "a religion," "a national religion," "a particular religion," or "a particular denomination." Rather, it says, "Congress shall make no law respecting an establishment of religion." Thus, "it is religion generically that may not be established."[8]

Therefore, the text prohibits government from making any law respecting an establishment of religion—any and all religions! Nor can government prohibit the free exercise of religion—any and all religions! And no religion can use its political influence upon government to establish itself socially in a favored position over other religions.

(8) The Supreme Court ruled in numerous decisions over an extended period of time that the First Amendment should be interpreted in terms of church-state separation. Since *Everson vs. Board of Education* (1947), a tradition of interpretation revolving around the philosophy of separation has been produced. The appeal to Thomas Jefferson's separationist interpretation goes back much further, as far as 1878 in the Supreme Court decision *Reynolds vs. United States*, which quoted Jefferson's "Letter to the Danbury Baptists" containing the phrase "wall of separation" and then stated:

> Coming as this does from an acknowledged leader of the advocates of the measure, it may be accepted almost as an authoritative declaration of the scope and effect of the amendment.

Even earlier, in *Watson vs. Jones* (1872), the Supreme Court had declared:

> In this country the *full and free* right to entertain *any* religious belief, to practice *any* religious principle, and to teach *any* religious doctrine which does not violate the laws of morality and property, and which does not infringe personal rights, is conceded to all. The law knows no heresy, and is committed to the support of no dogma, *the establishment of no sect.*[9]

Rejection of church-state separation for a nonpreferentialist or majoritarian-accommodationist philosophy cannot be justified by appeals to a nonpreferentialist, accommodational "original intent" (there was no single such intent by which to define the meaning of the First Amendment). It should be recognized for what it is—a profoundly illiberal, majoritarian exercise of judicial activism on the part of justices who claim that they oppose such activism!

Decisions such as *Employment Division vs. Smith* (1990) and the recent (1997) overturning of the Religious Freedom Restoration Act have, in the opinion of many, gutted First Amendment protection of religious liberty. It is now permissible for state and local governments to enact laws and policies that prohibit the free exercise of minority religions and to grant special recognition, preferences, and privileges to majority religions!

In addition, rejection of a principle and tradition of interpretation like that of church-state separation, which is well established socially and historically, is an exercise in political radicalism—not of conservative political method. Consistently carried out, the destruction of the constitutional "wall of separation" between church and state that has begun with recent Supreme Court decisions will result in further diminishment of and threats to religious liberty. Radical religionists, with the aid of radical, majoritarian justices and courts, might well proceed with radical agendas for promoting a "Christian America" and subvert the religious liberty of all who do not share their radical politics and religion.

Taken together, the preceding eight facts of constitutional origin and interpretation justify the conviction that church-state separation is in fact a constitutional assumption and principle. Exactly how church-state separation is to be applied to specific issues of religious liberty and relations between religion and government may be disputed among separationists themselves, and will certainly be disputed by anti-separation accommodationists and theocrats. But the fact that church-state separation, properly understood and applied, is a requirement of religious liberty and constitutional jurisprudence cannot be justifiably denied.

Discussion Questions

1. How significant is the fact that "God" and religion were not appealed to in the Constitutional Convention of 1787 or in the text of the Constitution?
2. Discuss the quotation of James Madison on page 21, note 5. Do you agree or disagree with this statement by the Father of the Constitution and author of the Bill of Rights?
3. What is right or wrong with nonpreferential government support of all religions? What are the potential benefits and possible dangers?
4. Is advocacy of church-state separation a "liberal" or a "conservative" position? Why?

Notes

[1]Rick Scarborough, *Enough Is Enough: A Call to Christian Commitment* (Springdale PA: Whitaker House, 1996) 65.

[2]David Barton, *The Myth of Separation: What Is the Correct Relationship Between Church and State?* (Aledo TX: Wallbuilder Press, 1992) 41, 45, 46.

[3]James Madison, *Notes of Debates in the Federal Convention of 1787* (New York: W. W. Norton, 1987) 234.

[4]Quoted in Isaac Kramnick and R. Laurence Moore, *The Godless Constitution: The Case Against Religious Correctness* (New York: W. W. Norton, 1996) 105-106.

[5]Letter from James Madison to Edward Livingston, quoted in Robert Alley, *James Madison on Religious Liberty* (Buffalo NY: Prometheus Books, 1985) 83.

[6]See Leonard Levy, *The Establishment Clause: Religion and the First Amendment* (New York: Macmillan, 1986) and Douglas Laycock, " 'Nonpreferential' Aid to Religion: A False Claim about Original Intent," *William and Mary Law Review* 27 (1986), for decisive scholarly refutations of the assertion that the original intent of the First Amendment allowed nonpreferential aid to religion (or Christianity) in general, based upon the history of the adoption of the First Amendment in the First Congress.

[7]Douglas Laycock, "Original Intent and the Constitution Today," in *The First Freedom: Religion and the Bill of Rights*, ed. James E. Wood, Jr. (Waco TX: J. M. Dawson Institute of Church-State Studies of Baylor University, 1990) 92.

[8]Ibid., 99.

[9]Emphasis added.

Chapter 3

An Ideal in Search of a Metaphor

Church-state separation is undeniably a constitutional assumption and principle. However, the question remains as to *how separate* church and state should be. Contrary to the view of strict or maximal separationism (the more separation, the better!), the view that the Constitution requires absolute or maximally strict separation between religion and government is as much an error as is the notion that church-state separation is a lie and that the United States was constituted as a Christian nation.

The worldview myth of "Secular America" that underlies at least some accounts of strict separationism also distorts historical evidence and betrays an ideological mindset and agenda. As the Williamsburg Charter states:

> Justifiable fears are raised by those who advocate theocracy or the coercive power of law to establish a "Christian America." While this advocacy is and should be legally protected, such proposals contradict freedom of conscience and the genius of the Religious Liberty provisions. At the same time there are others who raise justifiable fears of an unwarranted exclusion of religion from public life. . . . Interpretations of the "wall of separation" that would exclude religious expression and argument from public life, also contradict freedom of conscience and the genius of the provisions.[1]

The myth of secular America functions for its adherents and proponents, individually and communally, in ways that are similar to the function of the myth of Christian America for the Religious Right. It also engenders false accounts of the historical relations between religion and politics and between religion and government, and promotes what Richard John Neuhaus has famously termed "the naked public square."[2]

For some, the myth of secular America encourages proposed strategies of church-state separation that can only be described as expressions of an agenda of antireligious bigotry and intolerance. Thomas Flynn, for instance, evidenced a radical and hostile view of church-state separation when he wrote:

> I believe the surest precondition for real religious freedom in *private* life is the removal of religious language, symbols, and subject matter from *public* life. If there is a broad enough religious diversity within the body politic, the peaceful carrying on of public life and public debate will necessarily require environments from which religious divisiveness has been wholly removed. . . . If we wish to protect a certain area from religious divisiveness, we must first cleanse it of religion itself.[3]

While Flynn's views are extreme and idiosyncratic and do not represent mainstream separationist views and strategy, one may nevertheless sense that Flynn's sentiments and wishes are shared by at least some few militant secularists among church-state separationists. It is unfortunate that such hostile and persecutorial sentiments and agendas are too often identified with church-state separationism itself by accommodationists or leaders of the Religious Right who have a vested interest in creating straw separationist monsters by which to mobilize their following.

A militantly secular, radically separationist philosophy and strategy, based upon the myth of secular America, would allow for little, if any, public and governmental accommodation of religion. Does this myth really offer itself as a myth of origins—what we were or are as Americans—or as the myth of a future secular utopia what we should be as America? Yet, governmental accommodation of religion, religious institutions, and public religious expression has been widely practiced (sometimes legitimately, but quite often illegitimately) to one degree or another in the history of American society and politics.

Even strict separationists like Thomas Jefferson and James Madison found it neither possible nor desirable to pursue *maximally strict* or absolute church-state separation. The Supreme Court decisions in

Zorach vs. Clauson (1952) and *Wisconsin vs. Yoder* (1972) were, in fact, accommodationist decisions, although as such they were anomalies in comparison to other Supreme Court decisions of the era.

Accommodation of religion by the state may be constitutional in particular circumstances, also due to the fact that, according to Justice William O. Douglas,

> The First Amendment . . . does not say that in every and all respects there shall be a separation of church and state. It studiously defines the manner, the specific ways, in which there shall be no concert, union, or dependency one upon the other. That is the common sense of the matter. Otherwise, the state and religion would be aliens to each other—hostile, suspicious, even unfriendly.[4]

If such is the case, why do some separationists insist upon and persist in the notion—apart from intellectually pathological reasons such as those evidenced by Thomas Flynn—that church-state separationism must be maximally strict or more-than-less absolute in character?

A major influence upon the philosophy and agenda of strict or absolute church-state separation—which would allow very little or no accommodation of religion by the state—has been Thomas Jefferson's metaphor of a "wall of separation" between church and state, the imaginative power of which has sparked and guided much interpretation of the First Amendment. The mental picture this metaphor creates encourages the view that just as a wall completely separates property on either side of the wall, so church and state can be completely separated. Such a picture of complete church-state separation is an evidently monstrous view when critically evaluated on historical and sociological grounds, if not also philosophically.

Jefferson's inadequate and misleading wall metaphor of church-state separation must either be critically qualified, or it should be abandoned. Though it has represented an important social and constitutional concern and point—that of church-state separation and non-establishment—it has also caused great misunderstanding as to what is possible and desirable in matters of church-state relations. Church-state separation, as Justice Douglas recognized, is not the same as a total divorce of religious values, persons, or all religiously-motivated agendas from the political process and from government and governmental institutions. Yet it is not easy to come up with a better metaphor than Jefferson's wall metaphor!

In the foreword to this book James Dunn affirms the continued propriety of some type of "barrier metaphor" for church-state separation and mentions a barbed-wire-fence metaphor of church-state separation. This metaphor deserves more attention than that paid to a merely off-hand illustration. In Texas, where I have lived all of my life, barbed wire fences are regarded with some degree of respect and care. They are erected for a purpose, a part of which is to warn against, and to impede, passage and trespass between certain areas.

Barbed wire fences are far from impregnable or impassable barriers, for one may with some care go over, under, or through them, and one may do so for good reasons. The specific location of a barbed wire fence may not be an infallible indication of where the line of separation between properties actually exists, and the particular location of the fence may be more pragmatically than legally based. A fence might require repositioning if challenged as to its pragmatic value or legal standing.

Nevertheless, one ought to proceed with caution before, during, and after deciding to traverse a barbed wire fence. There are, or at least were, good reasons for that fence's being placed where it is. It is a good assumption that one should not pass through such barriers without appropriate justification. One should also recognize that any such decision to circumvent a barbed wire fence may carry very real risks and costs. So it is with church-state separation.

The ideal of church-state separation warns of the dangers of connection and union between Augustine's "City of God" and the "City of Man." It reminds both religion and government that they are differing spheres of practice and authority within the providence of God and that both function best when there exists between them what William O. Douglas describes as less "concert, union, or dependency."

Perhaps a more relational and less material metaphor than the traditional barrier metaphor might be of service, such as a "troubled marriage metaphor" of church-state separation. Married couples who have legally separated or divorced still find themselves with many significant, unavoidable, and desirable points of contact with, and accommodation to, one another. These points of contact and accommodation are, of course, often fraught with peril if used by either party to gain advantage over the other.

While circumstances may dictate that separation is the wisest course of action in some troubled marriages and also in church-state relations—and any "marriage" of church and state is going to be at best a troubled marriage!—legal separation or divorce in either case cannot mean a total personal and social separation—either of two individuals or of two social institutions such as church and state.

Separation of church and state has never meant and cannot mean or require the total divorce of religious persons, values, and agendas from the public sphere or the political arena. And it must be vigorously stressed that the public and governmental spheres of society are not synonymous! There are important, unavoidable, and sometimes desirable points of contact and accommodation between church and state that make maximal, absolute, or strict separation unfeasible and undesirable.

Yet, as Thomas Jefferson, James Madison, and Justice Douglas recognized, "concert or union or dependency" between church and state is dangerous both to the freedom and integrity of religion and to the freedom and integrity of government. While some contact and accommodation are inevitable and acceptable, accommodation should be minimal, instituted only when necessary, rather than maximal, or established whenever desired.

The greatest degree of separation possible, up to the point at which excessive separation in the name of nonestablishment threatens legitimate free exercise claims and practices, should be the presumption and norm. The power of religious institutions, sectarian religious ideologies, and religio-political agendas have historically proven to be great threats to civil and religious liberty. Yet the power of governmental institutions and "secularism-ic" political ideologies and agendas may also threaten religious liberty, either though an excessive application of church-state separation in the cause of non-establishment, or through an excessive state-church accommodation (of majoritarian religion) in the cause of free exercise.

It is both a politically inevitable and necessary consequence of the content of the religion clauses of the First Amendment that there will be tension and occasional conflict between implementation of the Free Exercise Clause by state-church accommodation and implementation of the Non-Establishment Clause by church-state separation. Jefferson's wall metaphor is totally unsuited to expressing this tension and potential conflict within the First Amendment. To the extent that use of the wall metaphor of church-state separation obscures or leads interpreters of the First Amendment to dismiss this tension and potential conflict between free exercise/accommodation and non-establishment/separation, is the extent to which the wall metaphor misleads First Amendment jurisprudence and policies of separationism or accommodationism.

Also, to the extent that the wall metaphor of church-state separation leads interpreters of the First Amendment to believe that religion and government can actually be hermetically sealed off from one another is the extent to which barrier metaphors such as the wall metaphor are inadequate and need replacement. But is there a metaphor that can more adequately serve the ideal of church-state separation?

Discussion Questions

1. Does church-state separation require the exclusion of religious persons, values, and beliefs from society or the democratic political process?
2. What do you think of Thomas Jefferson's "wall metaphor" of church-state separation? What are its strengths and weaknesses?
3. In what ways is entanglement between religion and government like a bad marriage? What are the problems and dangers of church-state entanglement?
4. Can there be a more-or-less absolute or strict separation between church and state? Should there be?

Notes

[1]"The Williamsburg Charter," in *Articles of Faith, Articles of Peace: The Religious Liberty Clauses and the American Public Philosophy*, ed. James Davison Hunter and Os Guinness (Washington DC: Brookings Institution, 1990) 136.

[2]See Richard John Neuhaus, *The Naked Public Square*, 2d ed. (Grand Rapids: Eerdmans, 1984). Chapter 14, "The Morality of Compromise," should be required reading for every ideologue in church-state debates, left and right, accommodationist and separationist.

[3]Thomas Flynn, "The Case for Affirmative Secularism," *Free Inquiry* (Spring 1996): 12, 16.

[4]*Zorach vs. Clauson* (1952).

Chapter 4

The Myth of
"Christian America"— Part 1

Since the Supreme Court decision *Everson vs. Board of Education* (1947), the guiding principle for the interpretation of the religion clauses of the First Amendment has been that of the separation of church and state. Court decisions have determined that no Christian church or denomination should be established as a national church or receive preferential treatment by government over other Christian bodies. Moreover, the Supreme Court has held that no Christian institution can receive preferential treatment by the government over other non-Christian religions. Nor can state or local governments prefer Christianity or any other religious body over other religions or over those who profess no religion at all.

Traditionally, many Christian bodies have been staunch advocates of church-state separation. Notable among such bodies have been the Baptists. The *Baptist Faith and Message*, revised and re-adopted by the Southern Baptist Convention in 1963, states:

> God alone is Lord of the conscience, and he has left it free from the doctrines and commandments of men which are contrary to his word or not contained within it. Church and state should be separate. The state owes to every church protection and full freedom in the pursuit of its spiritual ends. In providing for such freedom no ecclesiastical group or denomination should be favored by the state more than others. . . . The church should not resort to the civil power to carry on its work. The gospel of Christ contemplates spiritual means alone for the pursuit of its ends. The state has no right to impose penalties for the religious opinions of any kind. The state has no right to impose taxes for the support of any form of religion. A free church in

a free state is the Christian ideal, and this implies the right of free
and unhindered access to God on the part of all men, and the right
to form and to propagate opinions in the sphere of religion without
interference by the civil power.

Recently the doctrine of church-state separation has come under
attack from advocates of a "Christian America" among some fundamentalist and evangelical Christians and groups who have been politically mobilized into the Religious Right. They assert that the phrase
"separation of church and state" is not contained within the text of the
Constitution. They argue that it is an unsound interpretation, if not a
contradiction of, the [sic] "original intent" of the First Amendment
that has been foisted upon the Constitution by modern-day secularists
and activist Supreme Court judges. Rick Scarborough charges: "When
the Supreme Court Justices ruled that the Constitution erected a 'wall
of separation' between church and state, they lied."[1]

A purportedly-true story of the Constitutional Convention of 1787
is often offered as a demonstration that the Founding Fathers did not
practice or intend church-state separation. The story is held to demonstrate, on the contrary, that the Founding Fathers sought to institute a
specifically Christian nation, directly and primarily based upon
Christianity and its doctrines. The story goes something like this:

The Convention was hopelessly divided and at an impasse and
crossroads. It was facing self-destruction over heatedly disputed issues
such as the method of representation in the new Senate. At the height
of the crisis Benjamin Franklin eloquently called the Convention to
Christian prayer, which had previously been omitted by the delegates.
Members of the Convention, deeply moved and convicted by Franklin's speech, approved Franklin's motion, and subsequent meetings
were begun with official prayer. A religious revival of sorts broke the
impasse and established fraternity and cooperation between the delegates. In renewed dependence upon God and biblical precepts, this
"prayer meeting convention" subsequently produced a Constitution
based upon the doctrines of the Bible and of Christianity, and it
instituted the United States as a Christian nation.

Advocates of Christian America assert that biblical and Christian
teachings directly and determinatively influenced the political
thought, and deliberations, and the resulting Constitution of 1787.
They claim that specifically Christian motives and goals were at work

in the efforts of the delegates at nation-building, and that public prayer and pious dependence upon God during the Convention demonstrate that church-state separation was not their intent and is in fact a false story foisted upon constitutional origins by modern-day secular humanists.

It is important to recognize that there are at least two meanings of the word "myth." (1) It is a "false story." (2) It is a narratively embodied worldview. David Barton uses the word "myth" in the first sense of the word—to charge that church-state separation is a false story of the origins and meaning of the Convention, the Constitution, and the First Amendment in the First Congress. But, in fact, the story of the prayer meeting Convention is a false story concerning the proceedings of the Constitutional Convention of 1787—an easily and embarrassingly demonstrable falsehood. Moreover, at least as Rick Scarborough defines and uses the word, the charge that church-state separation is a lie is, in reality, a lie!

In addition, the notion of Christian America that underlies and motivates this false story functions as a myth in the second sense of the word—as a worldview that has been embodied in a historically false narrative of constitutional origins. The notion that our nation was founded primarily and directly upon the Christian religion as a specifically Christian nation is used by members of the Religious Right to rationalize a particular view of how (some fundamentalist/evangelical) Christianity and civil government should relate in our nation. It is employed to justify maintenance or pursuit of a socially and governmentally preferred and privileged position within society of (some fundamentalist/evangelical) Christianity over other religions and nonreligious citizens.

Now it cannot, or should not, be denied that the Christian religion, through its moral and religious teachings and its cultural influences, was a significant personal influence upon the delegates to the Constitutional Convention of 1787, and thus indirectly upon the Constitution they crafted. Yet, evangelical Christian scholars Mark Noll, Nathan Hatch, and George Marsden have acknowledged the difficulty that exists for present-day conservative Christians in understanding the religious convictions of the Founding Fathers:

The difficulty arises because these brilliant men, surely the most capable generation of statesmen to ever appear in America, were at once genuinely religious but not specifically Christian. Virtually all these great men had a profound belief in "the Supreme Judge of the World" and in "the protection of Divine Providence," to use the words of the Declaration of Independence. Yet only a few believed in the orthodox teachings of traditional Christianity.[2]

Some of the early American leaders were devout Christians, such as Benjamin Rush and John Witherspoon. None, except for Thomas Paine and Ethan Allen, were publicly anti-Christian. But many of those leaders were unorthodox in their religious views, though they kept those thoughts to their diaries and letters to other gentlemen. According to evangelical Christian historian Steven J. Keillor,

> Their unorthodoxy they derived from . . . the Moderate (mostly English) Enlightenment, not from cynical amoral French skeptics whose views were unacceptable to most Americans. American evangelicals were slow [and still are!] to detect this private Deism.[3]

Gary Scott Smith is a contemporary Christian "reconstructionist" scholar and no friend of church-state separation. In contrast to advocates of the founding of our nation as a "Christian America," Smith recognizes that there was no distinctively Christian political understanding during the colonial period. As the new nation was formed, it was built upon an eclectic foundation, not simply and solely upon Christian and biblical principles. He holds that "our nation has never been thoroughly or consistently Christian."[4]

Russell Kirk, a "paleo-conservative" scholar, and again no friend to church-state separation, judged in his helpful work *The Roots of American Order*:

> The roots of [American] order twist back to the Hebrew perception of a purposeful moral existence under God. They extend to the philosophical and political self-awareness of the old Greeks. They are nurtured by the Roman experience of law and social organization. They are entwined with the Christian understanding of human duties and human hopes, of man redeemed. They are quickened by medieval custom, learning, and valor. They grip the religious ferment of the sixteenth century. They come from the ground of English

liberty under law, so painfully achieved. They are secured by a century and a half of community in colonial America. They benefit from
the debates of the eighteenth century. They approach the surface
through the Declaration and Constitution. They emerge full of life
from the ordeal of the Civil War.[5]

It would therefore be at best a monstrous oversimplification, and is
in actuality a falsehood (and one without any scholarly excuse for its
espousal) to assert that the Founding Fathers were acting specifically as
Christians in their efforts to found our nation and that their intent was
to create a "Christian nation" through their efforts. It is plainly a false-
story myth of our national origins.

We must recognize that David Barton and his fellow advocates of a
Christian America are the myth-makers with regards to Constitutional
and First Amendment origins and interpretation. In fact, some assertions are merely expressions of wishful and mythical thinking. An
example is this comment by Tim LaHaye: "Were George Washington
living today, he would freely associate with the Bible-believing branch
of evangelical Christianity [fundamen- talism!] that is having such a
positive influence upon our nation"[6] But according to evangelical
scholar John Warwick Montgomery, "Only extreme naiveté or invinci-
ble ignorance can claim that the chief midwives at our nation's birth
were representatives of the classical Christian tradition."[7] The view
that the Founding Fathers of our nation were fundamentalist Christians in wigs and knickers is plainly, laughably, and dangerously false.

It is important to document that not only political-theological liberals and secular humanists, but also political-theological conservatives
and evangelical Christians reject the false and historically irresponsible
contention that America was founded as a Christian nation.
Montgomery notes,

> In certain circles of the far right of the religious spectrum it is cus-
> tomary to wax eloquent on the "Bible religion of our Founding
> Fathers.". . . Though we might fervently wish that these sentiments
> were accurate, the fact is that they express a pure mythology. The
> idea of believing Christian Founding Fathers is very largely a pious
> myth, and if we want to arrive at a balanced and mature understand-
> ing of the relation between scriptural religion and our national heri-
> tage, we must rigorously carry out a process of de-mythologization at
> this point.[8]

It is simply not the case that honest, competent, or authentically Christian scholarship will affirm that the United States was founded as a "Christian nation." In fact, exactly the opposite is true. Competent and honest scholarship—Christian or otherwise—recognizes the ambiguity, pluralism, and 'secularity' behind the efforts of our Founding Fathers to establish "a new order for the ages." The charge that church-state separation is a false-story myth of the origins and philosophy of the Constitution is itself a false-story myth!

Discussion Questions

1. What are some of the most significant evidences that support church-state separation as a constitutional philosophy and principle?
2. Re-read the quotation by Rick Scarborough on page 36, note 4. How does this statement square with the facts presented in this chapter?
3. Were the Founding Fathers of our nation "Christians"? In what sense of the word? Explain your response.
4. What does it mean to call the assertion that America was founded as a Christian nation a "myth"?

Notes

[1]See Rick Scarborough, *Enough Is Enough: A Call to Christian Commitment* (Springdale PA: Whitaker House, 1996) 83.

[2]Mark A. Noll, Nathan O. Hatch, and George M. Marsden, *The Search for Christian America* (Westchester IL: Crossway Books, 1983) 72.

[3]Steven J. Keillor, *This Rebellious House: American History and the Truth of Christianity* (Downers Grove IL: InterVarsity Press, 1996) 85.

[4]Gary Scott Smith, *God and Politics: Four Views on the Reformation of Civil Government* (Phillipsburg NJ: Presbyterian and Reformed Publishing Co., 1989) 4-5.

[5]Russell Kirk, *The Roots of American Order*, 3d ed. (Washington DC: Regnery Gateway, 1991) 472.

[6]Tim LaHaye, *Faith of Our Founding Fathers* (Brentwood TN: Wolgemuth and Hyatt Publishers, 1987) 113.

[7]John Warwick Montgomery, *The Shaping of America* (Minneapolis: Bethany House Publishers, 1981) 57.

[8]Ibid., 50-51.

Chapter 5

The Myth of
"Christian America"— Part 2

The Constitutional Convention of 1787 was in dire straits and in danger of dissolution when Benjamin Franklin made an appeal and a motion for public prayer within the Convention in an eloquent speech on the floor of the Convention on June 28, 1787. David Barton, in his book *The Myth of Separation*, assumes that the motion passed as a matter of course and asserts:

> Franklin's admonition—and the delegates' response to it—had been the turning point not only for the Convention, but also for the future of the nation. While neglecting God, their efforts had been characterized by frustration and selfishness. With their repentance came a desire to begin each morning of official government business with prayer . . . After returning God to their deliberations, were they effective in their efforts to frame a new government?[1]

However, as James Madison's notes on the Constitutional Convention demonstrate, dissension and debate broke out over Franklin's motion!

Alexander Hamilton and others expressed misgivings that the motion might bring on "some disagreeable animadversions" (heated disputes) and cause the public to believe that "embarrassments and dissension" within the Convention had brought on the motion.[2] One of the delegates pointed out that the Convention had no funds with which to pay a minister to offer prayers, even though, if David Barton is correct, local clergymen had volunteered to offer such prayers at no charge.[3] Edmund Randolph proposed an alternative motion that a special service be held on the Fourth of July at which time prayers would be offered. Franklin seconded Randolph's motion recognizing, as he later acknowledged, that the Convention "except for three or four persons, thought prayers unnecessary."[4] James Madison recorded in his notes that "after several unsuccessful attempts for silently postponing the matter by adjourning, the adjournment at length carried, without any vote on the matter."[5]

On July 2, following the purported (but non-actual) institution of official, public prayer in the Convention's proceedings that supposedly took place on June 29, the dissension within the Convention was still as heated and the division as deep as ever. Roger Sherman declared that "we are now at a full stop" and recommended that a committee work on the resolution of the issue of Senate representation.[6] On the same day Gouverneur Morris, one of the most influential delegates to the Convention, stated, "Reason tells us we are but men, and we are not to expect any particular interference from heaven in our favor."[7] (What a revealing statement this is, in contrast to the sentiments of Franklin and the assertions of David Barton!)

The dissension and impasse within the Convention continued long after the Convention rejected Franklin's call to prayer and after the observance of the Fourth of July religious service. On July 10 George Washington wrote to Alexander Hamilton:

> Our councils are now, it is possible, at a worse train than ever; you will find but little ground on which the hope of a good establishment can be formed. In a word, I almost despair of seeing a favorable issue to the proceedings of the Convention.[8]

On July 15 Caleb Strong summarized the Convention's situation: "The Convention has been much divided in opinion. . . . It is agreed on all hands [that] Congress [is] nearly at an end. If no accommodation takes place, the union itself must soon be dissolved."[9] Not until July 16 was the report of the committee, the so-called "Great Compromise," adopted, and only then was the impasse within the Convention broken —not on June 28 with Franklin's call and the Convention's nonexistent return to prayer and to God.

It is very significant that the Constitutional Convention began with no concern or provisions for official, public prayers as part of its proceedings. If the Founding Fathers were intent upon creating a new government based upon God and the Christian religion—a "Christian America"—how was such an omission possible? It would, in fact, be incomprehensible! Furthermore, how could the Convention reject Franklin's call to prayer if Barton's account of their intent is correct? In fact, it was not the case because the Founding Fathers were not out to create a Christian America.

James Madison's notes on the Convention irrefutably demonstrate that no official, public prayers were offered in the Constitutional Convention of 1787 at any time. When Benjamin Franklin proposed such prayers, his motion was not well received and was never brought to a vote. In a true expression of church-state separation, a religious service was held outside of the Convention on July 4 for those who wished to participate. The division and rancor of the Convention did not end until many days after the July 4 religious service, when a compromise concerning representation in the new United States Senate was reached. If a "miracle" took place in the Convention, it was not the result of official, public prayer or the introduction of God into the deliberations of the delegates.

Furthermore, neither the preamble nor the body of the Constitution that resulted from the work of the Convention make any appeal to religious motives or authority. The only substantive mention of religion within the text of the Constitution is present in Article Six, Clause Three in the rejection of any religious tests for holding office in the new national government. All other religious references, for example, "in the year of our Lord 1787," are incidental and ceremonial.

Again, these facts are simply incomprehensible if the Founding Fathers intended to create a Christian America by their efforts to formulate a new federal Constitution. First Amendment scholar Leo Pfeffer observed that it is very significant that the Constitution as it emerged from the Constitutional Convention of 1787 contained no references to or invocations of God. This was in marked contrast to pronouncements of the Continental Congress.

> The omission was not inadvertent; nor did it remain unnoticed. . . .
> At a meeting of Congregationalists in June 1788 a request was presented "that some suitable Testimony might be borne against the sinful omission in the late Federal Constitution in not looking to God for direction, and of omitting the mention of the name of God in the Constitution.[10]

Timothy Dwight, an evangelical Christian and the president of Yale University at the time of the founding generation, declared some time after the Convention:

> The Nation has offended Providence. We formed our Constitution without any acknowledgment of God; without any recognition of His mercies to us as a people, of His government, or even of His existence. The [Constitutional] Convention, by which it was formed, never asked, even once, His direction, or His blessings, upon their labors. Thus we commenced our national existence under the present system, without God.[11]

Harold O. J. Brown, a contemporary advocate of the establishment of (rather than "return" to) a Christian America, echoes Dwight's sentiments, charging that: "America made a mistake in 1787. Officially, government (the Federal government first, later all the states) broke with Christianity."[12] Similarly, Walter Berns states: "If the Founders had intended to establish a Christian commonwealth . . . it was remiss of them—indeed, sinful of them—not to have said so and to have acted accordingly."[13]

There were repeated attempts during the nineteenth and early twentieth centuries to introduce appeals to God and Jesus Christ into the text of the "Godless Constitution" by constitutional amendment. Generation after generation of "Christian Americanists" recognized the lack of religious rationale or motive in the text of the Constitution and sought to remedy the deficit. Only in recent years have some evangelical/fundamentalist Christians of the Religious Right adopted a new tactic to promote a Christian America. They attempt to import a religious and Christian intent into the text and history of the Constitution that is not there, and that previous generations had the good interpretive sense and clarity of historical insight to recognize is not there.[14]

How may one explain the manifest falsehoods and apparent incompetence and incomprehension in the use and interpretation of historical sources that one finds evidenced by those who promulgate the false-story myth of the "prayer meeting convention" and the false-story myth of the Founding Fathers' intent to create a Christian America? Such an explanation may be found, at least in part, through understanding a second sense of the term "myth"—as narratively embodied worldview.

Worldview myths order the experience of an individual or a group of people. They constitute and empower individual and group identity. They provide ideological direction for the practical—and political—activities of the individual and the group. A worldview myth, particularly when it serves a power interest and becomes an ideology, can distort one's perceptions and interpretations of fact and historical evidence. According to Mircae Eliade,

> Myth is always related to a "creation"; it tells how something came into existence . . . By knowing the myth one knows the "origin" of things and hence can control and manipulate them at will; . . . Myth fulfills . . . an indispensable function; it expresses, enhances, and codifies belief; . . . [It is] a pragmatic charter of primitive faith and moral wisdom.[15]

The myth of Christian America is in part a creation myth or a myth of origins. It offers an explanation and a meaning of the American nation for the present-day "heirs" of the Founders' "Christian America." This worldview myth also reconciles religious allegiances to both church and state on the part of the Religious Right by means of a fundamentalist-style civil religion. According to William Lee Miller,

> There is an understandable impulse on the part of the pious segment of the American populace to get its two pieties lined up: Bible and Constitution, disciples and founders, God and country. But it leads to a distorted and misleading picture of our national past. And that distortion is more consequential than others, because the founding has mythic and narrative power for Americans . . . In the long run, across the whole culture, that interpretation cannot prevail—the interpretation, that is, that insists upon religion as the necessary foundation of America's republican institutions.[16]

The worldview myth of Christian America that seeks to line up the two pieties of the Religious Right has its roots in the religious origins of the Plymouth and Massachusetts Bay colonies and in the Puritan vision of America as a "city on a hill" and a "light to the nations."[17] This vision was widely present within the minds and hearts of many early Americans, but was already fading in its cultural influence at the time of the Constitutional Convention of 1787. Christians in the Religious Right still identify with this vision, explanation, and meaning of America. They hold that their Christian America is the true America and that they are the true Americans.

Because America is, according to the tradition and worldview of the Religious Right, a Christian nation, and because Christians are the true Americans, the historical origins of the nation in the Constitutional Convention must have been specifically, primarily, and directly Christian. The Founding Fathers must have been essentially like themselves—"true Americans" or (evangelical/fundamentalist) Christians. The success of the Constitutional Convention in the midst of difficulties must have been due to the intervention of God. The world view and myth of origins of the Christian Americanists cannot and does not allow them to see things any other way, and thus generates a false-story myth of the Constitutional Convention. They must therefore "earnestly contend for the nation once and for all delivered unto the saints!"

Also, because of the way things must have been, Christian Americanists of the Religious Right believe that they are the true Americans and theirs is the true America. One should note the deductive historiography and circular reasoning inherent in such a view. E. M. Adams has rightly criticized those "who write about events for the purpose of promoting some theory or ideology. They interpret events in terms of the theory or ideology in question and then use the events involved as support for the theory or ideology."[18]

The practice and espousal of such a deductive and circular interpretation of history is due to the fact that, according to Adams,

> There is a strong tendency to read the past in a way that not only explains the present but legitimizes it and provides direction for the future. When this tendency is not rigorously held in check, preconceived theories and the purposes of justification and edification dominate the search for, and interpretation of, the facts.[19]

There can be no better explanation of the creation of the false-story myth of the founding of Christian America than such a tendency, motivated by mythological and ideological thinking, that seeks to justify the present-day political agenda of the Religious Right.

The worldview myth held by the Religious Right distorts their investigation and interpretation of the evidence concerning the Constitutional Convention of 1787 and their understanding of the constitutional relationship between church and state. The Convention itself was an exercise in church-state separation. Its proceedings evidence a belief in and practice of the philosophy of church-state separation. It stands as a model for understanding and practicing church-state separation.

Religious Right myth-makers of a Christian America have clearly got their facts and interpretations of the Constitutional Convention, the Constitution, and the First Amendment wrong. The assertion of the "myth of church-state separation" is itself a mythic (ideological) and a mythical (false story) assertion and account of the origins and meaning of the Constitution and the American nation. To paraphrase David Barton, the denial of church-state separation as a constitutional principle is absurd; it has been repeated often, and people have (unfortunately) believed it!

Discussion Questions

1. How does awareness of the widespread use of demonstrably false statements and arguments like those of David Barton affect your views on the questions of America as a Christian nation and church-state separation?
2. Discuss the significance of Gouverneur Morris' statement on page 40, note 7: "Reason tells us we are but men, and we are not to expect any particular interference from heaven in our favor" for understanding the Constitutional Convention of 1787?
3. What original intent on the part of the Founding Fathers is revealed by the fact that no public prayers or religious arguments were offered in the creation of the constitution?
4. What does it mean to say that the claim that America was founded to be a Christian nation is a myth?

Notes

[1]David Barton, *The Myth of Separation: What Is the Correct Relationship Between Church and State?* (Aledo TX: Wallbuilder Press, 1992) 110. Barton's recent book, *Original Intent: The Courts, The Constitution, and Religion* (Aledo TX: Wallbuilder Press, 1996), corrects this representation of Franklin's

motion without acknowledging the error of his previous book. Barton has also published a list of "Questionable Quotes," several of which he had previously presented as historically authentic and upon which he had argued for the founding of the nation as "Christian America." Unfortunately, the previous misinformation is better known than Barton's corrections and qualifications. The damage done by this slipshod scholarship continues and is repeated on a wide scale.

²James Madison, *Notes of Debates in the Federal Convention of 1787* (New York: W. W. Norton, 1987) 210.

³Ibid. and Barton, 109-10.

⁴Quoted in Leonard W. Levy, *The Establishment Clause: Religion and the First Amendment* (New York: Macmillan, 1986) 64.

⁵Madison, 211.

⁶Ibid., 212.

⁷Ibid., 234.

⁸Quoted in Catherine Drinker Bowen, *Miracle at Philadelphia: The Story of the Constitutional Convention May to September 1787* (Boston: Little, Brown, and Co., 1966) 140.

⁹Madison, 293.

¹⁰Quoted in Leo Pfeffer, *Church, State, and Freedom* (Boston: Beacon Press, 1976) 122.

¹¹Quoted in Isaac Kramnick and R. Laurence Moore, *The Godless Constitution: The Case Against Religious Correctness* (New York: W. W. Norton, 1996) 105-106.

¹²Harold O. J. Brown, "The Christian America View," in *God and Politics: Four Views on the Reformation of Civil Government*, Gary Scott Smith, ed. (Phillipsburg NJ: Presbyterian and Reformed Publishing Co., 1987) 132.

¹³Walter Berns, "Religion and the Founding Principle," in *The Moral Foundations of the American Republic*, ed. Robert Horowitz, 3d ed. (Charlottesville VA: University of Virginia Press, 1986) 210.

¹⁴See Kramnick and Moore, 144-49 for an account of such recognition and attempts to amend the Constitution to rectify the situation.

¹⁵Mircae Eliade, *Myth and Reality* (New York: Harper Colophon Books, 1975) 20.

¹⁶William Lee Miller, "The Moral Project of the American Founders," in *Articles of Faith, Articles of Peace: The Religious Liberty Clauses and the American Public Philosophy*, ed. James Davison Hunter and Os Guinness (Buffalo NY: Brookings Institution, 1990) 35.

¹⁷It is very important to recognize that the origin of the American nation or of the various states in the United States does not date from the founding of the Plymouth and Massachusetts Bay colonies. According to Thomas

Jefferson and James Madison, the Declaration of Independence adopted (around) 4 July 1776 was "the fundamental act of union between the states." Abraham Lincoln agreed when he dated the founding of the nation in his "Gettysburg Address" of 1863 as "four-score and seven years ago." Others have held that the nation was not constituted until the adoption of the Articles of Confederation (1778) or, more widely held, until the ratification of the present Constitution in 1789. Efforts by Peter Marshall and others to make the founding and religious rationales of the Plymouth and Massachusetts Bay colonies the origin and rationale of the American nation are tendentious and unjustifiable attempts to read Christian and theocratic rationales into our system and institutions of government.

[18]E. M. Adams, *Religion and Cultural Freedom* (Philadelphia: Temple University Press, 1993) 41.

[19]Ibid., 42.

Chapter 6

The First Amendment, "Original Intent," and the Declaration of Independence

Do the religion clauses of the First Amendment guarantee religious liberty only to Christian churches and denominations, on a narrow, "original meaning" interpretation of "religion" in those clauses? David Barton evidently asserted such a view in his first, and most well-known book, *The Myth of Separation: What Is the Correct Relationship Between Church and State?* Interestingly, Barton's later book, *Original Intent: The Courts, the Constitution, and Religion*, contains arguments that are inconsistent with his narrow interpretation of the First Amendment and restrictive interpretation of religious liberty.

Barton affirms that the Constitution must be interpreted in light of the Declaration of Independence. He does so for the purpose of placing the "Godless Constitution"[1] into a religious and theological context. The Declaration refers to "the laws of nature and of nature's God" and holds that it is "self-evident, that all men are created equal and endowed by their Creator with certain unalienable rights." Barton rejects a legal positivism that constitutes an "abandonment of the transcendent biblical natural law principles" and that violates "the value system of 'the laws of nature and nature's God' established in the Declaration of Independence."[2] Barton notes that positivists believe the Constitution to be independent of the Declaration.

> This incorrect belief is of recent origin; in fact, it was rejected by earlier generations. . . . For generations after the ratification of the Constitution, the Declaration was considered a primary guiding document in American constitutional government. In fact, well into the twentieth century, the Declaration and the Constitution were considered as inseparable and *inter*dependent—not independent—documents.[3]

In the Declaration, the Founders established the foundation and the core values on which the Constitution was to operate; it was never to be interpreted apart from those values.[4]

The Founding Fathers did, in fact, believe that there is an objective world order, created by God, that consists of natural laws of morality and public polity, along with natural laws of science. They held that there are rights that any just and proper government is required to recognize and to secure, "among which are life, liberty, and the pursuit of happiness." The wording of the Declaration evidenced the Founders' belief that there are other recognized and recognizable natural rights beyond those stated in the Declaration.

Part of the original intention of the Constitution-makers was to protect rights and to limit government—not to protect (majoritarian) government and limit (minority) rights. The Ninth and Fourteenth Amendments to the Constitution also recognize the existence of natural rights not enumerated in the Bill of Rights, whose failure of enumeration did not constitute a denial of their existence, the necessity of their protection, nor of their relevance for constitutional interpretation.

Thus, on Barton's own premises of the nature of the Declaration of Independence and of natural rights, the fact that a claimed right or the proposed extension of a right is not contained or enumerated within the text of the Constitution of 1787, the Bill of Rights, or the state constitutions appealed to by Barton for "the original intent"[5] of the First Amendment does not mean that such a right does not exist or cannot come to be recognized as a right by subsequent interpreters and interpretations of the Constitution. It does not mean that such rights, upon their recognition and protection, have been invented or created by judges and courts because they are not in the Constitution. Recognition of unenumerated rights or new extensions of rights that are enumerated in the Constitution—going beyond any "original intent" of the Founders—may be seen as justified by the text and logic of the Declaration of Independence and its principle of equality and equal rights for all citizens of the United States.

The relevance of the Declaration of Independence for constitutional interpretation and jurisprudence should not be quickly dismissed. Thus, the importance of "natural rights" (or "universal human rights," in modern parlance) for constitutional interpretation also should not be dismissed. The Declaration, while bearing the imprint of the mind of Thomas Jefferson, was also the product of a committee of the Continental Congress, was adopted by the entire Continental Congress, and represented widespread views held by the American people.[6]

Because its assumptions, views, and logic were widely held, they are of great importance for understanding how the Constitution was understood in the founding generation. They are useful for continued direction of the American experiment and for any discussions of "original intent" or "original meaning" of the Constitution. The assumptions, content, and logic of the Declaration are useful now, as in previous American history, in guiding progressive interpretation of the Constitution and, particularly, of the First Amendment religion clauses.

One may well argue, as does Charles L. Black, that the Ninth and Fourteenth Amendments "incorporate" the Declaration of Independence, its stated natural rights of "life, liberty, and the pursuit of happiness," and its recognition of other unenumerated natural rights.[7] Even if the Declaration is not recognized to have the force of law by incorporation, it should be recognized as vital historical background to interpreting the Ninth Amendment's affirmation of "other rights retained by the people." Therefore, any claim concerning original intent or original meaning or any status quo interpretation of the Constitution that violates the spirit and substance of the Declaration should be recognized and discarded as unconstitutional.

As a case in point, the Founding Fathers evidently did not originally intend to include African-Americans among the "all men" who are endowed by their Creator with the "unalienable rights" of "life, liberty, and the pursuit of happiness." Slavery was not universally originally intended or originally understood to be disallowed by the Declaration of Independence or the Constitution of 1787. However, a number of the Founding Fathers either personally recognized that African-Americans should be accounted as equal human beings possessing "unalienable" rights, or, at least, that there was a logic expressed in the Declaration that raised the issue of the natural justice of involuntary servitude imposed upon a particular race of persons.[8]

In his moral and political opposition to slavery, Abraham Lincoln appealed to the text of the Declaration and its affirmation that "all men" are created equal and endowed with equal "unalienable" rights. Advocacy of the expansion of civil rights to African-Americans beyond the original intent of the Founding Fathers was exemplified in Lincoln's vision. As Gary Wills argues in his Pulitzer Prize-winning book, *Lincoln at Gettysburg: The Words That Remade* America, Lincoln's views on the priority of the Declaration of Independence for the interpretation of the Constitution helped to define further the meaning of the Constitution and of the American nation.[9]

Abraham Lincoln, following the constitutional philosophy of James Wilson, Joseph Story, and Daniel Webster, held that the Declaration was a statement of a permanent ideal of which the Constitution was a particular, time-conditioned embodiment. The substance and interpretations of the Constitution must continually be tested in light of the ideal of equality in liberty and brought into continually closer approximation to that ideal.[10] Lincoln declared,

> They [the fathers who issued the Declaration] meant to set up a standard maxim for free society, which should be familiar to all, and revered by all; constantly looked to, constantly labored for, and even though never perfectly attained, constantly approximated, and thereby constantly spreading and deepening its influence, and augmenting the happiness and value of life to all people of all colors everywhere.[11]

Regarding those who would today dispute such a "declarational" interpretation of the Constitution by Lincoln and his successors, or turn back constitutional interpretation and restrict its protection of rights in the name of an "original intent" radicalism,[12] we should recognize with Wills that:

> The Gettysburg Address has become an authoritative expression of the American spirit—as authoritative as the Declaration itself, and perhaps more influential, since it determines how we read the Declaration. For most people now, the Declaration means what Lincoln told us it means, as a way of correcting the Constitution itself without overthrowing it. . . By accepting the Gettysburg Address, its concept of a single people dedicated to a proposition, we have been changed. Because of it, we live in a different America.[13]

In opposition to the mythology of original intent, it should also be recognized, as constitutional scholar Jack Rakove asserts, that:

> Both the framing of the Constitution in 1787 and its ratification by the states involved processes of collective decision-making whose outcome necessarily reflected a bewildering array of intentions and expectations, hopes and fears, genuine compromises and agreements to disagree. . . . In this context, it is not immediately apparent how the historian goes about divining the true intentions or understanding the roughly two thousand actors who served in the various conventions that framed and ratified the Constitution, much less the larger electorate they claimed to represent. . . . The notion that the Constitution had some fixed and well-known meaning at the moment of its adoption dissolves into a mirage.[14]

Nevertheless, in contrast and contradiction to Lincoln's views, Robert Bork has written that "the Declaration's pronouncement of equality was sweeping, but sufficiently ambiguous . . . The ambiguity was dangerous because it invited the continual expansion of the concept and its requirements."[15] Bork recognizes the pragmatic importance of the moral assumptions of the Founding Fathers for the public moral discipline of the individual in the exercise of her constitutional rights. He laments the increasing disappearance of those assumptions and personal moral limits from American society. He holds that those personal and public moral assumptions and values have functioned, and need to function, as extraconstitutional, *de facto* limits upon the exercise of liberty by individuals.

Bork also appears to hold that, insofar as those assumptions influenced the original meaning of the Constitution, those assumptions also function as *de jure* limits upon the interpretation, limits, and exercise of rights today—given that, in his mistaken view, "original meaning" is the only valid guide to what rights are recognized and protected in the Constitution.[16] But for Abraham Lincoln, and those who did and do not subscribe to Bork's brand of legal positivism, the natural law language and logic of the Declaration of Independence do not merely invite, but require the expansion of the principle of equality and the extension of natural rights of "life, liberty, and the pursuit of happiness" to those who were not originally intended to be included as recipients of such rights and protections.

Robert Bork does not wish to allow that the language and logic of the Declaration may be used to justify the expansion of rights and their requirements to contemporary situations not envisioned or originally intended by the Founding Fathers. He bemoans the "subjective," "arbitrary," "unprincipled" character of any such process and decisions, and their relativization of the "objective, strictly-constructed-according-to-original-intent-and-meaning" Constitution he advocates. He wants the moral assumptions of the Founding Fathers restored in personal and social life, assumptions that were natural law assumptions to a significant extent, but not as substantive guides and justifications of progressive constitutional interpretation.

David Barton likewise asserts that individual texts contained within the Constitution may be interpreted in light of a single, specifiable original intent or original meaning that is to be strictly constructed. Thus, he believes that the original meaning of the First Amendment was to allow nonpreferential aid to, and religious liberty protection of, Christian denominations only. In his espousal of a constitutional hermeneutics of original intent or meaning, he is in agreement with Robert Bork.

However, David Barton's position on the significance of the Declaration of Independence and natural law for constitutional interpretation contradicts that of Robert Bork. In advocating the Declaration's priority to and organic relationship with the Constitution, Barton unwittingly undermines his contention that only denominations of Christianity are subjects of the free exercise and non-establishment protections of the First Amendment.

The Declaration of Independence may well be seen as an informing and reforming force and standard in constitutional interpretation. Extensions of Constitutional or "Declarational" rights to persons and to groups beyond those originally intended for inclusion should be recognized as constitutional by the courts and the people. This the Supreme Court has done in extending the right and protection of religious liberty to persons and religions beyond Christian denominations, beyond narrow interpretation of religion in the First Amendment, and beyond narrow views of original intent.

As Justice William Brennan wrote in *Abington School District vs. Schempp* (1963),

Our religious composition makes us a vastly more diverse people than were our forefathers. They knew differences chiefly among Protestant sects. Today the Nation is more heterogeneous religiously, including as it does not only substantial minorities of Catholics and Jews but as well of those who worship according to no version of the Bible and those who worship no God at all. In the face of such profound changes, practices which may have been objectionable to no one in the time of Jefferson and Madison may today be highly offensive to many persons, the deeply devout and nonbelievers alike.[17]

In conclusion, no religion should or can have its free exercise prohibited by government or by oppressive religious factions manipulating the political process in the effort for quasi-establishment of their religion. The status, statements, assumptions, and logic of the Declaration of Independence preclude such. And no religion—not even Christianity—may pursue preferential recognition, privileges, or support by government, not even when rationalized by (spurious) appeals to original intent. The Constitution, interpreted correctly and in light of the Declaration of Independence, guarantees religious liberty to all religions and for all American citizens.

Discussion Questions

1. The Declaration of Independence states that *all* persons possess "unalienable rights" of life, liberty, and the pursuit of happiness and that governments are instituted to secure such rights. How should this guarantee impact our interpretation of the First Amendment's religious liberty provisions?
2. Are state governments and majority votes in state legislatures sufficient protection of religious liberty for all Americans? Do you agree with Abraham Lincoln or with Robert Bork on the significance of the Declaration of Independence for affirming and protecting individual rights and liberty? Why?
3. How has our federal system of government, involving the national and state governments, changed since 1787? What do these changes mean for our interpretation of the Constitution and the First Amendment's religious liberty clauses?

Notes

[1]See Isaac Kramnick and R. Laurence Moore, *The Godless Constitution: The Case Against Religious Correctness* (New York: W. W. Norton, 1996), for a competent and spirited defense of this description.

[2]David Barton, *Original Intent: The Courts, the Constitution, and Religion* (Aledo TX: Wallbuilder Press, 1996) 247.

[3]Ibid. For the sake of argument and brevity, this chapter will let pass the issue of whether or not Barton's summary and analysis are accurate.

[4]Ibid., 250.

[5]It is well nigh impossible to establish by historical investigation a single, unitary, universal, and monolithic original intent or original meaning for the Constitution as a whole or for the First Amendment in particular. In many cases in the constitutional text, and in the case of the First Amendment in particular, there were differing intents and meanings at work, depending upon the public involved.

[6]See Pauline Maier, *American Scripture: Making the Declaration of Independence* (New York: Alfred A. Knopf, 1997) chapter 3, for an account of the context of the creation of the Declaration.

[7]Charles L. Black *A New Birth of Freedom: Human Rights, Named and Unnamed* (New York: Grosset/Putnam, 1997).

[8]The issue of slavery, passed over by the Founding Fathers because of its political divisiveness, is an excellent example of diversity and limitations of moral perspective within the founding generation. The Declaration of Independence and the Constitution are time-relative (though not necessarily time-bound) documents, and their meanings are subject to the diversity, limitations, and compromises of perspective that characterized the original intentions of the Founding Fathers.

[9]Gary Wills, *Lincoln at Gettysburg: The Words That Remade America* (New York: Simon and Schuster/Touchstone Books, 1992). See also Maier, 208: No less than Thomas Jefferson, Abraham Lincoln gave expression to a powerful strain in the American mind, not what all Americans thought, but what many did. The values he emphasized . . . had, in fact, been part and parcel of the Revolution, and as much the subject of controversy then as later. Lincoln and those who shared his convictions did not therefore give the nation a new past or revolutionize the Revolution [in their interpretation of the Declaration of Independence].

[10]Wills, 101.

[11]Quoted in Wills, 102.

[12]One of the basic tenets of conservative social and political thought is that of incremental change. A spurious Barton-esque "return" to the original intent of the First Amendment would invalidate not merely decades, but

more than a century of the interpretation of the Constitution as a whole. Such a wholesale change can hardly be termed "conservative" and is indeed a radical proposal and agenda. Rejection of decades of well-established precedents in church-state matters, precedents that constitute a tradition of interpretation, would seem to be inconsistent with conservative stress upon the importance of tradition and the political community of past, present, and future. Radical change in First Amendment interpretation and the radical political and social consequences that might well follow are subject to the familiar conservative warning concerning "the law of unintended consequences." Furthermore, the fact that such an interpretive agenda is not in fact supported by "the" original meaning and intent of the First Amendment reveals that the agenda is rooted in ideological commitments and would constitute a blatant exercise in illiberal, majoritarian judicial activism!

[13]Wills, 146-47.

[14]Jack N. Rakove, *Original Meanings: Politics and Ideas in the Making of the Constitution* (New York: Random House/Vintage Books, 1997) 6.

[15]Robert H. Bork, *Slouching Toward Gomorrah: Modern Liberalism and American Decline* (New York: HarperCollins, 1996) 66-67. Note Bork's lamenting and disparaging use of the word "continually" in contrast to Lincoln's affirming and celebratory use of the word in the preceding quotation (note 13). Which of these two Americans is more worthy of our esteem and trust in interpreting the Constitution and our national character?

[16]Robert Bork may therefore be faulted on at least two major points: (1) his rejection of natural rights in favor of a legal positivist interpretation of the Constitution, and (2) his espousal of the mythology of a single original intent meaning behind the text of the Constitution that can and must be strictly constructed. For a masterful demolition of this view based upon the words and actions of the Founding Fathers, see chapter 1 of Leonard Levy's *Original Intent and the Framers' Constitution* (New York: Macmillan, 1988) and Rakove, *Original Meanings.*

[17]Douglas Laycock made a salient point with regard to Justice Brennan's observations when he wrote these words: "It is significant that the founders saw no problem with government sponsorship and endorsement of generic Protestantism. They saw no problem with it because in their society, no one complained. It did no apparent harm, no one raised the issue, and they had no occasion to seriously think about it. Just as the framers excluded blacks from the proposition that all men are created equal, they less consciously, less pervasively, and less cruelly excluded non-Protestants from the proposition that government should not establish religion. If a practice was not controversial among Protestants, it was not controversial at all. Government support for generic Protestantism is not evidence of what the Establishment

Clause means, because the founders were not thinking about the Establishment Clause when they did these things. . . . They did not seriously think about it, and so they had no intent for us to follow, and we must apply for ourselves the principle stated in the constitutional text." Douglas Laycock, "Original Intent and the Constitution Today," in *The First Freedom: Religion and the Bill of Rights*, ed. James E. Wood, Jr. (Waco TX: J. M. Dawson Institute of Church-State Studies, Baylor University, 1990) 103-104.

Chapter 7

The Religion Clauses
of the First Amendment

The First Amendment to the United States Constitution guarantees religious liberty for all citizens and prohibits any law that "establishes" religion (any and all religions) or prohibits the "free exercise" of religion (any and all religions). A law or governmental policy may be unconstitutional in one of two ways—if it violates the Free Exercise Clause or if it violates the Non-Establishment Clause.

An important question must be asked of the relation of the Free Exercise and Non-Establishment clauses of the First Amendment: Can they come into conflict in particular cases of church-state relations? Is there an inherent tension between the two religion clauses that sometimes issues forth in an outright conflict between governmental policy that would further free exercise at the risk of establishment of religion or that would disallow establishment of religion at the risk of prohibiting free exercise?

Leo Pfeffer, an ardent advocate of strict separationism in church-state relations, has long held that no tension exists between the two religion clauses and no real conflict can occur between governmental policy guaranteeing free exercise and governmental policy preserving non-establishment. Any purported conflict is more apparent than real, according to Pfeffer, for the concepts of establishment and free exercise are correlative and unitary.[1] In Pfeffer's words,

> The Fathers of the First Amendment were convinced that the free exercise of religion and the separation of church and state were two ways of saying the same thing: that separation guaranteed freedom and freedom required separation.[2]

Pfeffer opposes the view that there is tension and possible conflict between the non-establishment and Free Exercise clauses of the First Amendment because acknowledging such an opposition would encourage church-state accommodationists who argue that non-establishment is subordinate to free exercise in First Amendment jurisprudence. Such a view might privilege church-state accommodation—a view Pfeffer opposes—over church-state separation—the view Pfeffer advocates.

Pfeffer also apparently approves the view that "religion is a private matter."[3] Such a view of religious belief and practice impacts his assertion that there can be no true conflict between the religion clauses. It would seem that Pfeffer and some other strict separationists assume that there can be no conflict between non-establishment and church-state separation on the one hand, and free exercise on the other, for if religion is purely a matter of private belief and practice, governmental policy in a liberal democracy should not and does not as a matter of principle interject itself into such private matters.

For those with this privatistic view of religion, it would seem that when religious persons and institutions seek to exercise their religion in a social and activistic, rather than private way, they are not being authentically religious. Their public "free exercise" of religion must be separated from the governmental sphere and, for many, from the public square, due to the risk of violating other persons' public freedom from religion. Restrictions upon the public exercise of religion in the name of strict separationism are thus not held to be in conflict with or be an infringement upon the free exercise of ("true," i.e., "private matter") religion, because claims for accommodation of the public exercise of religion are not authentic religious or political claims.

Leo Pfeffer also appeals to the fact that the Supreme Court has affirmed that the religion clauses are "correlative and coextensive ideas"[4] and have failed in their decisions to pit the Free Exercise and Non-Establishment clauses against one other. In Pfeffer's own words, however, the Supreme Court has in fact "refused" to face a conflict between the Non-Establishment and Free Exercise clauses.[5] Such decisions "avoid rulings in which the Establishment and Free Exercise clauses can be played against each other."[6] Pfeffer suggests,

Although the Supreme Court has stated that there may be instances in which the establishment and Free Exercise clauses conflict with each other, the Court will continue to find ways to decide such cases without definitively adjudicating which clause is superior and which subordinate, or which must be preserved and which sacrificed.[7]

However, refusal by the Supreme Court to acknowledge conflicts between the religion clauses, avoidance of cases where such a conflict is evident, and finding ways not to definitively adjudicate which clause has priority over the other do not constitute an argument or a proof that there is no such conflict. They hardly indicate that, on a philosophical level, "the unity of the two clauses is accepted both by separationists and accommodationists on the Supreme Court."[8] In fact, such a willful approach to handling conflicts between the religion clauses testifies to the reality of such conflicts.

Barry Lynn has commented upon a strategy that the Supreme Court employs to avoid acknowledging and adjudicating the conflict that exists in many cases between non-establishment and free exercise. Where such a conflict is evident, yet where the Supreme Court wishes to decide in favor of religious liberty, the rationale of the Court's decision in favor of free exercise is not acknowledged to be that of the protection of free exercise. As in the case of *Widmar vs. Vincent* (1981), it is rationalized on the basis of the protection of free speech or equal protection of the laws and "not as a sufficient and independent basis for resolving a clash between governmental regulation and personal or corporate religious desire."[9]

Short of some crudely simplistic and absolute espousal that "the Constitution means what the Supreme Court says it means," the fact that the Court ducks religion clause conflict cases and decisions is no argument that no such conflicts do arise out of an inherent tension between free exercise and non-establishment. In fact, as Barry Lynn aptly summarizes,

> It is time to admit that the most polite thing one can say about the relationship between the two religion clauses in the First Amendment is that there is some tension between them. It would, however, be more accurate to acknowledge that they are essentially in direct conflict when it comes to religious exemptions from laws of general applicability, which is at the core of contemporary litigation.[10]

Insightfully, Lynn calls for a balancing of the Free Exercise and non-establishment clauses in situations where laws of general applicability impinge upon free exercise and raise the issue of religious exemptions from those laws—exemptions that then raise establishment concerns and issues. He rightly rejects any "talismanic method of resolving this conflict."[11] (See chapter 7 for further discussion and development of a dialectical approach to such conflicts.)

Derek Davis also recognizes that in cases where a government regulation that has been instituted for legitimate secular purposes penalizes or burdens religious conduct,

> . . . there arises an "ineluctable tension" between the two provisions of the First Amendment. On the one hand, the Court has said that the Establishment Clause forbids government action when the purpose is to aid religion, but, on the other hand, the Court has aid that the Free Exercise Clause may require government action to accommodate religion. In *Walz*, Chief Justice Burger conceded that the religion clauses "are cast in absolute terms, and either . . ., if expanded to a logical extreme, would tend to clash with the other.[12]

From a radically different perspective than that of Leo Pfeffer, Harvard law professor Mary Ann Glendon affirms the unitary and nonconflictive nature of the dual prohibitions of the First Amendment.[13] But Professor Glendon argues such unity on the basis that there is only one religious liberty clause—not two. She holds that non-establishment of religion is entirely subordinate in purpose to free exercise of religion and restricts activities of government, not those of religion. Thus, religious liberty and the First Amendment require accommodation of religion by the state, but not restrictions upon the "free exercise" claims of religion in the name of church-state separation.

According to Professor Glendon, free exercise requires maximal accommodation of religious activity on the part of the state. Free exercise of religion cannot be restricted by appeals to non-establishment or separation of religion from the state. Therefore, no restrictions upon governmental accommodation of religion in its "free exercise" can be justified by appeal to the Non-Establishment Clause or to church-state separationism.

Richard John Neuhaus concurs with Glendon's analysis: "The no-establishment provision of the Religion Clause is entirely in the service of the free exercise provision."[14] He argues that the Supreme Court has, in effect, subordinated the free exercise provision/clause to the non-establishment provision/clause in its church-state decisions over the past fifty years.[15] Furthermore, he holds that the proper interpretation of "the" religion clause recognizes its prohibitions as restrictions on government solely, and not upon religion.

However, Glendon's and Neuhaus' contention that there is only one religion clause seems a somewhat idiosyncratic and tendentious interpretation of the First Amendment. It is true that the literal grammatical form of the First Amendment may be taken to contain a single clause: "Congress shall make no law respecting an establishment of religion, nor prohibiting the free exercise thereof." But political documents often aim for an economy and felicity of style, and the substance and logic of religious liberty protection under the First Amendment consists of two prohibitions—no prohibitions of free exercise, no establishment of religion—and thus two concerns and two principles of protection of religious liberty. One concern/prohibition/protection is formally stated in a complete grammatical clause: "Congress shall make no law respecting an establishment of religion . . ." The second is expressed in shorthand: ". . . nor prohibiting the free exercise thereof."

It could well have been stated: "Congress shall make no law respecting an establishment of religion, nor shall Congress make any law prohibiting the free exercise of religion." But the present wording of the First Amendment would seem to be a more economical and felicitous rendering of these dual prohibitions. Implicitly, if not grammatically, the First Amendment contains two clauses, each expressing a differing prohibition in the service of religious liberty. Thus, whether or not the First Amendment should be read as containing two religion clauses, there is no doubt that two concerns, two prohibitions, and two provisions for protecting religious liberty are contained within the amendment. It ultimately matters little whether one speaks of two clauses or two provisions regarding religious liberty in the First Amendment.

Neither of the religion clauses/prohibitions should be seen or judged as either superior or subordinate to the other. Both are differing means to a common specific end—religious liberty—and ultimate end

—civil right. The ideal situation is one in which the two are consistent and correlative with each other in the service of religious liberty. The reality of the matter is that there is an inherent tension between the two, and they sometimes do come into conflict in particular cases.

However, Glendon's and Neuhaus' main point seems to be that the First Amendment religion clause(s) had and should be recognized to have a unitary intent to promote religious liberty, which they equate with "free exercise." The intent of the First Amendment definitely was not to separate church and state nor to prohibit establishments of religion as ends in themselves, or out of hostile or "secularism-ic" intent. Both free exercise—and thus accommodation of religion by the state—and non-establishment—and thus church-state separation—were intended to promote religious liberty, or as was sometimes more broadly stated and situated, "liberty of conscience."

However, Neuhaus in particular seems to discount the truth that religious liberty may require the state to protect itself from undue influence and control by religious majorities and institutions that, in the name of free exercise or accommodation, actually seek governmental preferences and privileges in ways not available for the free exercise of minority religions. In protecting itself from such influence and claims to free exercise and accommodation, the state protects the religious liberty of all religions.

Thus, church-state separation, and the freedom of government from religious institutions and their power, is necessary for free exercise of religion. Free exercise of (fanatical, authoritarian, and illiberal) religion that seeks for itself preferences and privileges not accorded to all religions and to all American citizens is not synonymous with religious liberty. Non-establishment may well at times have to trump such "free exercise" claims in order to preserve true free exercise and religious liberty for all.

Furthermore, as most persons' deepest convictions of conscience assumed a religious form in the time of the Founders, the terms "religious liberty" and "liberty of conscience" were virtually synonymous. Currently, however, deepest convictions of conscience may assume a religious, but nontheistic form, or even nonreligious forms grounded in secular humanism. Therefore, liberty of conscience and religious liberty are no longer synonymous terms and concepts, and the Supreme Court has correctly (and even in line with the Founders' evident "original intent"!) extended First Amendment religious liberty protection to those holding conscientious, but nontheistic and non-religion-based convictions.

Needless to say, non-theistic or secular humanistic convictions should not be established, preferred, or privileged within or by governmental institutions either. It is a major concern of the Religious Right (and often in the writer's opinion a valid concern) that the professedly secular (i.e., philosophically neutral toward religion, neither affirming nor denying specific religious convictions) character of governmental institutions has actually resulted in a clandestine preference for or quasi-establishment of secular humanist viewpoints.

It is interesting that the Supreme Court has adopted functional definitions of religion that include nontheistic and secular humanistic convictions for the purpose of free exercise rights, but has been reticent to apply the same functional definitions in its decisions regarding non-establishment. This lack of interpretive symmetry may have several motivations, possibly all salutary, but it only increases the concern of many religious persons that governmental institutions actually prefer and privilege the "religion" of secular humanism by guarding its free exercise but ignoring its potential violations of non-establishment. Some strict separationists do have such an intent and agenda and have acknowledged and welcomed this state of affairs.

Thomas Jefferson is usually referenced by those who advocate a unitary strict separationist First Amendment strategy as the paradigm spokesman and example of church-state separation in light of his famous "wall metaphor" of church-state separation. Jefferson's metaphor suggests a more or less absolute separation of church and state, with the church on one side of the social wall and the state on the other. Therefore, on the basis of the wall metaphor, many separationists assert that there is no conflict between the Non-Establishment Clause and the Free Exercise Clause, when both are identified with a strategy and policy of strict separationism.

Government takes care of its concerns on one side of the wall, and religion takes care of its concerns on the other side. Any seeming conflict that "appears" to require accommodation of religious expression is attributed to religion inauthentically and falsely trespassing the wall of separation. However, as Glenn Hinson claims,

Jefferson, along with many of this nation's founding fathers, was much influenced by the Enlightenment view that religion is "purely a private matter." To him separation meant the complete disengagement of the church from the state and the state from the church except through the private individual. He would not have envisioned the vast array of institutions that religious groups in America have developed to foster their diverse goals. Correspondingly, he would not have anticipated the many cases concerning church and state that have arisen almost exclusively from the institutional side of religion. . . . Because religion expresses itself institutionally, separation of church and state has meant reasonable or adequate rather than the absolute separation that Jefferson's phrase seems to imply. Separation is not equivalent to religious liberty.[16]

Jefferson, an anti-Federalist, also would not have anticipated the evolution of the federal union between the national and state governments into a more national system. He most likely would not have welcomed the growth in power of the judicial branch of government and its increase of authority and power in church-state matters. And Jefferson could not have anticipated the ubiquity of the bureaucratic/ regulatory state and the myriad ways in which it intersects with institutional religion in American society.

Add to all of these considerations the fact that Jefferson was not an absolute separationist at the federal level as president, and apparently much less so at the state level,[17] and one must conclude that the "wall metaphor" separation of church and state as advocated by some strict separationists today does not mean the same thing as Jefferson's "wall metaphor" separationism. Today's maximal or absolute separationism does not produce comparable religious and social consequences as it did in Jefferson's day. The consequence in today's society of attempting a policy of absolutely strict separationism is sometimes to restrict legitimate public expressions of religious liberty and thus come into conflict with the Free Exercise Clause of the First Amendment in the name of non-establishment.

Thus, there are new tensions and conflicts between free exercise and non-establishment due to the evolution of both state and church that Jefferson, Madison, and other Founding Fathers did not and could not have anticipated. It is anachronistic to unqualifiedly apply their (supposed) strict-absolute separation doctrine and practice to present social/political circumstances.

Even though church-state separationists are correct that separationism was a part of the original intent and the dynamics of the First Amendment, appealing to that strict separationist original intent as a trump card in complex and ambiguous circumstances of church-state intersection is neither consistent with many separationists' progressive views of constitutional interpretation nor appropriate or adequate to current circumstances and needs. There is an inherent tension within the First Amendment between free exercise of religion, and thus state-church accommodation, and non-establishment and church-state separation. In cases of conflict between the two clauses/prohibitions and their attendant strategies, neither can invariably be preferred over the other.

Discussion Questions

1. Do you think there is a tension between the two religion clauses of the First Amendment and their respective guarantees of "non-establishment" and "free exercise" of religion? Why? In what ways do conflicts arise?
2. Is religion primarily a private matter, or is it significantly and necessarily public in character? What should happen when religion and government meet in the "public square"?
3. Does government sometimes need to protect itself from religion in order to guarantee religious liberty? Why or why not? If your answer is yes, in what ways should the government protect itself?
4. How helpful a philosopher and model-maker of church-state relations is Thomas Jefferson in your view?

Notes

[1]Leo Pfeffer, *Church, State, and Freedom*, 2d ed. (Boston: Beacon Press, 1967) 139. Pfeffer admits five times in two pages of text that there are situations in which the dual prohibitions of the First Amendment may "appear" to conflict. He states: "The conflict may be more apparent than real. . . . It is, however, true that in most cases the conflict appears irreconcilable, and that it is a difficult task to determine where 'establishment' ends and 'free exercise' begins. The difficult task of drawing lines and weighing apparently conflicting values is not unique in the subject under study in this volume; it can hardly

be avoided in any area of constitutional law." In this quotation Pfeffer seems to recognize and struggle with a conflict that is, in fact, more real than apparent! Given this admission, Pfeffer's advocacy of strict separationism appears subject to the charge of irrationality discussed in chapter 8, note 3.

[2]Leo Pfeffer, "The Unity of the First Amendment Religion Clauses," in *The First Freedom: Religion and the Bill of Rights*, ed. James E. Wood, Jr. (Waco TX: J. M. Dawson Institute of Church-State Studies, Baylor University, 1990) 133.

[3]Pfeffer, *Church, State, and Freedom* 132.

[4]Justice Wiley Rutledge, opinion in *Everson vs. Board of Education* (1947).

[5]Pfeffer, "The Unity of the First Amendment Religion Clauses," 155.

[6]Ibid., 160.

[7]Ibid., 140.

[8]Ibid., 160.

[9]Barry W. Lynn, "The Sad State of Free Exercise in the Courts," in *The Bill of Rights: Original Meaning and Current Understanding*, ed. Eugene W. Hickok, Jr. (Charlottesville VA: University Press of Virginia, 1991) 71.

[10]Ibid., 79.

[11]Ibid.

[12]Derek Davis, *Original Intent: Chief Justice Rehnquist and the Course of American Church/State Relations* (Buffalo NY: Prometheus Books, 1991) 118.

[13]Mary Ann Glendon, "Religion and the Court: A New Beginning?" in *Religious Liberty and the Supreme Court: The Cases That Define the Debate over Church and State*, ed. Terry Eastland (Grand Rapids: Ethics and Public Policy Center/Eerdmans, 1993) 476-77.

[14]Richard John Neuhaus, "The Public Square: 'We Hold These Truths'—An Argument to be Engaged," *First Things* (November 1997): 69.

[15]There is some substance to Neuhaus' charge, at least with reference to more recent rulings concerning the constitutionality of moments of silence within public schools.

[16]E. Glenn Hinson, *Religious Liberty: The Christian Roots of our Fundamental Freedoms* (Louisville KY: Glad River Publications, 1991) 114.

[17]See Daniel Driesbach, "A New Perspective on Jefferson's Views on Church-State Relations: The Virginia Statute for Establishing Religious Freedom in its Legislative Context," *The American Journal of Legal History* 35 (1991): 176-204.

Chapter 8

Religious Liberty and Church-State Separation

In his famous essay, "The Will To Believe," philosopher William James insightfully introduced two strategies one may follow in belief adoption: (1) seek to gain truth, or maximize the true beliefs one holds, or (2) seek to avoid error, or minimize the false beliefs one holds. James rightly noted that these options are not the same strategy under different descriptions. They do not share the same epistemic priorities and fears; both strategies assume epistemic risks, but differing ones. They differ in how they apply the benefit of the doubt and the burden of proof to controversial proposals for belief, and in their intended results and unintended consequences. The priorities, epistemic fears, acceptable risks, benefits of the doubt, burdens of proof, and intended and unintended results may be illustrated as follows:

	Gain Truth Strategy	Avoid Error Strategy
Belief Priority	Maximize True Beliefs	Minimize False Beliefs
Epistemic Fear	Rejection of Truth	Acceptance of Error
Acceptable Risk	Acceptance of Error	Rejection of Truth
Benefit of the Doubt	Given to Some "Insufficiently Justified" Belief Proposals	Not Given to "Insufficiently Justified" Belief Proposals
Burden of Proof	Less Strict	More Strict
Intended Result	More True Beliefs	Fewer False Beliefs
Unintended Result	More False Beliefs	Fewer True Beliefs

It is especially significant that the epistemic fear of the gain truth strategy (rejection of truth) is the acceptable risk of the avoid error strategy, while the epistemic fear of the avoid error strategy (acceptance of error) is the acceptable risk of the gain truth strategy. Since the acceptable risk of the gain truth strategy is the acceptance of error, the benefit of the doubt is given to proposals for belief whose evidentiary backing is not sufficient to compel belief and the burden of proof required of such proposals is not very strict. In contrast, since the acceptable risk of the avoid error strategy is the rejection of some belief proposals that may in fact be true but that have insufficient evidential backing to compel belief, the burden of proof placed upon such proposals is stricter, and no benefit of the doubt is given in such circumstances.

Because the two strategies do not share the same epistemic priorities and fears, and do not embrace the same commitments to risk, they are not likely to produce agreement as to what proposals for belief should be accepted as true and which should be rejected as false in matters that are ambiguous and disputed.

William James' belief strategies may be adapted and applied to matters of religious liberty and church-state relations. There are two strategies one may follow in pursuit of religious liberty that have their source in the religion clauses of the First Amendment. One may seek to maximize "free exercise" of religion through governmental accommodation of institutional religion, or one may seek to minimize "establishments" of religion through maximal or strict separation of institutional religion and government.

Further complicating the issue is the fact that "free exercise" and "non-establishment" are not necessarily understood in the same way by their advocates and opponents. One person's free exercise of religion may well be seen by another person as an establishment of religion, while the other person's non-establishment may well be a prohibition of free exercise of religion in the view of the former person. There is no noncontroversial set of necessary and sufficient conditions by which to define and to distinguish between "free exercise" and "non-establishment" of religion. Much disagreement in church-state matters stems from ambiguity and equivocation in the use of these terms.

Church-state accommodationism and church-state separationism are differing religious liberty strategies and do not evidence the same attitudes and values or produce the same results in matters of church-state relations. One may seek to promote free exercise through governmental accommodation of religious institutions and activities, at the risk of going too far in one's accommodationism and supporting establishments of religion. Or one may seek to avoid establishments of religion through church-state separation, at the risk of going too far in one's separationism and prohibiting free exercise of religion. Due to the ubiquitous presence of government in American society, expressions of institutional religion will inevitably have to be either accommodated by, or separated, from governmental institutions and authority in its legislative, executive, judicial, regulative, and welfare functions. The only way to pursue religious liberty while avoiding or reducing issues of governmental accommodation of, or separation from, religion would be to reduce government's presence in, and control of, "the public square."

The values, fears, accepted and unaccepted risks, recipients of benefits of doubt and burdens of proof, and intended and unintended results of the two religious liberty strategies of accommodationism and separationism differ drastically and may be illustrated as follows:

	Accommodation	Separationism
Religious Liberty Priority	Maximize "Free Exercise"	Minimize "Establishments"
Greater Concern/ Unaccepted Risk	Restrict "Free Exercise"	Promotion of "Establishments"
Lesser Concern/ Accepted Risk	Promotion of "Establishments"	Restriction of "Free Exercise"
Benefit of the Doubt	Given to Disputed Accommodationist Policies	Given to Disputed Separationist Policies
Burden of Proof	Placed upon Separationist Policies	Placed upon Accommodationist Policies
Intended Result	More "Free Exercise"	Fewer "Establishments"
Unintended Result	More "Establishments"	Lesser "Free Exercise"

People who genuinely care about religious liberty are concerned with inappropriate restrictions upon the free exercise of religion *and* inappropriate establishments of religion. They desire as much free exercise of religion and as few establishments of religion as possible. They deplore excessive establishments of religion and deficient free exercise of religion. However, there is no single strategy that enables them to gain all they value or to avoid all they disvalue, and they differ in what they value and in what concerns them *most* in these matters.

Some persons value the greatest possible degree of free exercise and are concerned most about perceived threats to free exercise of religion. Others value freedom from the imposition of others' religion upon their free exercise of religion and are most concerned with perceived threats of religious establishments. Because they differ in their greater values and concerns in matters of religious liberty and church-state relations, persons will differ as to what risks they are willing to assume in their pursuit of optimum religious liberty: whether it be the risk of supporting objectionable restrictions upon free exercise by excessive policies of church-state separation or the risk of supporting objectionable establishments of religion by excessive policies of church-state accommodation.

Because of the perceived risks and threats of the religious liberty strategy they do not follow, and often because of a lack of appreciation of the risks and threats to religious liberty contained within their chosen strategy, persons will differ as to where the benefit of the doubt and the burden of proof are to be placed in questionable issues, circumstances, and policies. The benefit of the doubt will be given to their policy views and the burden of the proof placed upon the policy proposals of the competing strategy. Separationists will give the benefit of the doubt to separationist policies and the burden of the proof to accommodationist proposals. Accommodationists will give the benefit of the doubt to accommodationist policies and place the burden of proof upon separationist proposals.

Persons will differ as to the degree to which church-state separation or state-church accommodation should be instituted in society, or the degree to which government and religion should be separated from one another and the degree to which religion and government should accommodate each other. For the strict separationist, if it is not necessary to accommodate religion, it is required to separate religion and government. For the accommodationist, if it is not necessary to separate religion and government, it is required for government to accommodate religion. People will differ in these matters and strategies because they differ in what they value most: the maximization of free exercise (freedom for [their own?] religion) or the minimization of establishments (freedom from [other people's] religion).

In times of social and cultural stability, security, and confidence, advocates of free exercise may feel safe in accepting a separationist religious liberty strategy that preserves the political status quo, resists further state-church accommodation, and neither increases nor decreases free exercise. But in times of social and cultural instability, insecurity, and anxiety, in which the status quo in church-state relations is deemed flawed and free exercise is being challenged by new restrictions placed upon religious expression in the name of non-establishment, advocates of free exercise may become more concerned to preserve and to promote their free exercise through the advocacy of state-church accommodation. They may come into political conflict with church-state separationists who seek to change the status quo of state-church accommodation and quasi-establishments of religion or to preserve the separationist, non-establishment status quo.

Conflict between advocates of free exercise and state-church accommodation and advocates of non-establishment and church-state separation is understandable, unavoidable, and politically desirable in a democratic constitutional republic. Richard J. Neuhaus comments,

> Politics is a multifaceted, complex process that requires a weighing of concerns and interests in the hope of mutually tolerable compromise. . . . various interests and concerns are kept in play only because particular groups in the political process give highest priority, even exclusive attention, to narrow agendas. We can and should aspire to advance a comprehensive concern for the common weal. But every individual and every group is shaped by a world that is but a slice of the whole. Within those worlds particular hopes and discontents assume an urgency that may not be felt by others. In addition to the inevitable partiality of our experience, there are times in which we deliberately choose to accent one concern that otherwise might be neglected in the larger mix we call the political process. Democracy depends upon countervailing forces, and those who place what we think is an inordinate acent on one issue are essential to sustaining the democratic enterprise.[2]

Because of the inevitability and desirablity of difference in strategy and substance between accommodationists and separationists in the pursuit and preservation of religious liberty, each may avoid demonization and vilification of the other by recognizing and understanding the other in terms of their special religious liberty strategy with its differing values, concerns, and accepted political risks. The separationist may recognize that the accommodationist is not necessarily an enemy of the Constitution, and the accommodationist may recognize that the separationist is not necessarily an enemy of religion!

Civility between disputants in church-state controversies may be promoted by recognition of the two conflicting religious liberty strategies and the partial validity and political necessity of the strategy that one does not follow. Humility may be promoted by recognition that one's own religious liberty strategy is partial and assumes special and disputable values and risks.

It must be recognized that neither religious liberty strategy is sufficient for religious liberty of itself and neither strategy is infallible. Either one, of itself, will inevitably result in mistaken and excessive church-state policies and arrangements if it dictates political policy by itself.[3] There is no third "meta-strategy" available to adjudicate between the two strategies in particular conflict cases or to instruct the jurist or legislator when to choose one strategy's policy conclusion over the other.

The religion clauses of the First Amendment require that strategies of both church-state separation and state-church accommodation be advocated in the cause of religious liberty. Both non-establishment separationism and free exercise accommodationism must provoke, qualify, and restrict the implementation of the other. There are no easy formulas or sufficient rules of political reasoning by which philosophically pure or consistent court decisions and legislation may be attained that will be satisfactory to all.[4] Practical and dialectical thinking, rather than absolutist and ideological thinking, is required. Compromise between, and harmonization of, the competing values of free exercise/accommodation and non-establishment/separation will be necessary in disputed matters of the relations between institutional religion and government.

Discussion Questions

1. Which strategy do you follow in your decisions about what to believe or not to believe? How does your favored belief strategy impact your political and church-state views?
2. Which religious liberty strategy seems best to you in deciding matters of church-state relations? What risks do you assume in affirming and practicing your religious liberty strategy?
3. Do you see people who disagree with you politically as helpful and necessary to the democratic process and the pursuit of the common good? How should your answer influence your attitudes, actions, and reactions toward those who disagree with you politically?
4. How serious an error would it be if church-state accommodationism had absolute sway in a Christian America? How serious an error would it be if strict church-state separation had its way in a secular America?

Notes

[1] As introduced and exemplified by his classic essay, "The Will to Believe."

[2] Richard John Neuhaus, *The Naked Public Square: Religion and Democracy in America*, 2d ed. (Grand Rapids: Eerdmans, 1984) 47-48.

[3] It is, in fact, *irrational* to think that the cause of religious liberty can be served by maximizing either church-state separation in the cause of non-establishment or state-church accommodation in the cause of free exercise. Nicholas Rescher argues: "Rationality consists in the intelligent pursuit of appropriate ends. Now this is unquestionably a matter of selecting 'the best option' among alternatives: it calls for so comporting oneself in matters of belief and action as to prefer what is preferable—what deserves to be preferred. But when this preferability cannot be quantified, when its determination is a matter of qualitative judgment rather than quantitative measurement, then *rationality ceases to be a matter of maximization*. . . . Rationality is a matter of opting for the best available alternative. But there is simply *no way of transmuting this "best" into "the most of something."* See *A System of Pragmatic Rationality*, vol. 2, *The Validity of Values* (Princeton NJ: Princeton University Press, 1993) 39. Emphasis added.

[4] The desire for or conviction that there must be a single principle or formula that will yield a singularly valid, objective, and sufficient judgment resolving specific issues of church-state relations betrays "foundationalist" epistemic presuppositions and manifests itself in a foundationalist "mood and rhetoric." Foundationalism in epistemology (theory of knowledge) holds that

there exist absolutely objective, universal, noncontextual and supratraditional foundational truths that justify all contingent, situational beliefs. Foundationalism is increasingly recognized as a chimera in philosophical inquiry. Yet, some strict separationists—who subordinate free exercise claims to non-establishment values—and some maximal accommodationists—who subordinate non-establishment claims to free exercise values—often speak as though their religious liberty principle/strategy is the single, absolutely objective, universally valid, sufficient truth by which religious liberty can be defined and discerned. And it is often assumed that anyone who disputes such a status given either to separationism or accommodationism is either ignorant, perverse, or both. Rodney Clapp cautions: "Nothing is gained by resorting to the foundationalist mood and rhetoric. In fact, foundatonalist rhetoric actually makes conversation and conversion more difficult, since it inclines us toward believing that those who disagree are necessarily benighted or ill-intentioned. And who of us tries to listen to someone who regards us a stupid or immoral?" See "How Firm a Foundation: Can Evangelicals Be Nonfoundationalists?" in *The Nature of Confession: Evangelicals and Postliberals in Conversation*, edited by Timothy R. Phillips and Dennis K. Okholm (Downer's Grove IL: InterVarsity Press, 1996) 90.

Chapter 9

Wisdom,
the Elusive Factor
in Political Controversies

The so-called "Serenity Prayer" could more aptly be termed the "Wisdom Prayer." The politically engaged of whatever ideological persuasion, whether conservative or liberal, would do well to reflect upon it carefully. "God, grant me the serenity to accept the things I cannot change, the courage to change the things I can, and the wisdom to know the difference." In light of the increasing polarization and hostility between conservatives and liberals within American society, and the accompanying culture wars America is experiencing in the struggle to define its future,[1] such a prayer, taken to heart, may provide a transforming perspective on the insights and inadequacies of the ideologies of conservative social preservationism and liberal social progressivism.

The first line of the prayer, in its desire for the serenity to accept unchangeable things, may be seen as speaking to the special need of liberals who favor progressive social change. It reminds liberals that there are things in our society and polity that cannot or will not change much, if at all. Liberals often seem to forget that there are also many things that should not be changed in society; change would not be for the better, but for the worse. Conservatives are correct in their view that we live in a world that is tragically imperfect. Our knowledge, wisdom, and power to effect change have both practical and inherent limits. Liberals cannot be assured that the intended consequences of progressive political efforts will, in fact, result, or that unintended, negative consequences will not be the result of those efforts and policies.

It seems evident from history that some liberal-progressive policies and programs have resulted in negative, unintended consequences in both past and present. Society has sometimes suffered from miscon-ceived and misguided progressive policies and programs. It is inevitable that liberals will make errors in judgment and seek to change things that as a matter or principle or fact should not be changed. Or they will be frustrated in their efforts to effect progressive change due to human and social resistance and limitations.

Conscientious liberals recognize and accept the risk and inevitabil-ity of error and are willing to accept the political and social guilt that such mistakes and their consequences incur. These liberals exhibit the courage to change the things they can, according to their best under-standing of the world and their chosen (liberal/progressive) social/political strategy. But in the face of the inevitable frustrations and fail-ures of their efforts to change the status quo, liberals may well seek a spiritual serenity that accepts their inability to effect salutary change and acknowledges the ultimate and inherent inadvisability of some of the changes they greatly desire. "God, grant me the serenity to accept the things I cannot change" is a prayer of, and for, spiritual and political wisdom on the part of ideological liberals.

On the other hand, the second line of the prayer, in its desire for courage to change the things that one can, may be seen as speaking to the special need of conservatives/preservationists. It may remind them that there are things in our society and polity that should and can be changed for the better. There are things conservatives do not recognize that can and should be changed. Change can be for the better and not for the worse overall. Liberals are correct in their view that we live in a world of hope and opportunity in which we often do have the knowl-edge, wisdom, and power to effect beneficial change. It cannot be assumed that disastrous, unintended consequences will be the result of any particular policy or program of liberal/progressive reform or that the intended salutary results of such efforts cannot or will not in fact eventuate.

Conservatives of the past opposed changes in society that ulti-mately proved to be both achievable and beneficial. In fact, the para-dox of modern conservatism is that present-day conservatives often seek to preserve that which was the result of liberal/progressive policies and programs of the past, which conservatives of the past opposed. Conscientious conservatives recognize and accept the inevitability of error and are willing to accept the political and social guilt that such mistakes and their consequences incur.

78

In the face of inevitable frustrations and failures in their efforts to conserve/preserve the status quo, conservatives may well seek and benefit from courage to accept change and acknowledge the ultimate and inherent advisability of social and political change. "God, grant me the courage to change the things I can" is a prayer of, and for, spiritual and political wisdom on the part of the ideological conservative.

Both conservatives and liberals pursue their visions of the common good, but from differing perspectives regarding change and the status quo. Their respective sociopolitical strategies may be illustrated thus:

	Conservative/ Preservationist	Liberal/ Progressive
Political Priority	Preserve Status Quo/ Past Political Solutions	Change Status Quo/ Past Political Solutions
Political Fear	Gain New Political Errors	Lose New Political Solutions
Acceptable Political Risk	Lose New Political Solutions	Gain New Political Errors
Benefit of Doubt	Given to Conservative Policies	Given to Liberal Policies
Burden of Proof	Given to Liberal Policies	Given to Conservative Policies
Intended Political Result	Preserve Old Solutions/ Fewer New Errors	Gain New Solutions/ Fewer Old Errors
Unintended Political Result	Preserve Old Errors/ Fewer New Solutions	Gain New Errors/ Fewer Old Solutions

Both conservative and liberal political philosophies and strategies assume risks in possible harms to society and to individuals in their opposition to, or advocacy of, change. Problems arise because conservatives are sometimes too serene (timid) in preserving the status quo in relation to possible change. Likewise, liberals are sometimes too courageous (foolhardy) regarding change in relation to the status quo. Thomas Oden points out:

The *conserving mind* rightly prizes the past, values achievements hard won from the long history of morality, reflection, political struggle, and cultural transformation. The *progressive mind* rightly prizes the future of truth, and especially values the potential new insights that promise to correct long-held errors and obsessions. Each struggles against a different temptation to become excessive: The conserving view may *over*value established views, making an idol out of past achievements and misjudging the capacity of dated forms to sustain themselves amid the emerging challenges of history. The progressing view may *under*value the inheritance of the past and too avidly imagine that the future holds unparalleled truth and values of which the past is thought to be totally ignorant.[2]

What is often lacking in our society and politics today is "the wisdom to know the difference" between those things that should be changed and those things that should be conserved. The weakness in wisdom of liberal/progressive ideologues lies in recognizing the things that cannot or should not be changed. The weakness in wisdom of conservative/ preservationist ideologues lies in recognizing those things that can and should be changed. It is probably not possible for any one person, political group, or agenda to embody such "wisdom to know the difference" within itself—not even if they are moderate or pragmatic rather than ideologically conservative or liberal. There is no strategy or formula that can capture such transcending "wisdom to know the difference," hence the appeal and necessity of the lesser and partial wisdoms—ideologies—of conservatism and liberalism.

Nevertheless, our Founding Fathers were wise beyond the appreciation of either present-day ideological conservatives or ideological liberals in providing a political system in which both liberal and conservative political philosophies and strategies play a necessary role through their creative opposition to one another. Ours is a political system in which liberalism and conservatism check, balance, and sometimes win out over one another, and in which the damage that might be done if either were to exercise political and social hegemony is limited by the presence and opposition of the other. It is a system whose results will often frustrate and dissatisfy both ideological conservatives and liberals. Yet it may well provide the best approximation to "the wisdom that knows the difference" in that it recognizes, accommodates, and balances political agendas and actors who most often neither possess nor practice such wisdom.

If our society cannot transcend the internecine warfare and incivility between ideologues of the Right and the Left, we will continue to antagonize each other and to polarize our nation in cultural warfare. Hostility may well escalate—as it has in certain cases in the abortion conflict—to the point of standing over or hiding the bodies of one's opponents.

We need to recognize and appreciate the ambiguity and complexity of life that our political philosophies and strategies encounter. We need to recognize the weaknesses and errors of ideological thinking in response to this complexity and ambiguity. In the first chapter of the third volume of his *Systematic Theology* titled "Life and its Ambiguities," Paul Tillich insightfully discussed the ambiguities of life and the challenge they present to the human spirit. He held that culture is a manifestation of spirit, including our social and political institutions and philosophies. The effort of spirit towards integration sometimes necessitates the sacrifice of the actual for the possible or of the possible for the actual. Every such sacrifice, according to Tillich, involves a moral risk. The moral life of spirit requires such risking, but such risks "must be taken with the awareness that it is a risk and not something unambiguously good on which an easy conscience can rely."[3]

The often-timid soul of the conservative prefers the risk of loss of the possible to loss of the actual. The often-foolhardy soul of the liberal prefers the risk of loss of the actual to loss of the possible. In the ambiguities of social existence, the risk of sacrificing important and realizable possibilities to actual imperfections, as well as the risk of sacrificing important realities to inadvisable or unrealizable possibilities, can be equally great. Every moral and political decision is a risk because there are no guarantees that our political decisions will serve justice (or "the law of love," according to Tillich).[4]

Ideological conservatives and liberals need to take to heart the risks that their respective ideologies and political strategies entail. They are prone to self-deceived easy consciences that view their political values and philosophies as the truth, the whole truth, and nothing but the truth. Too often both liberals and conservatives refuse awareness of bias that distorts and frustrates all efforts for justice in society. As Daniel Heliminiak comments,

Because of bias, we attend assiduously to certain things and overlook others; we do not think to question some beliefs but completely dismantle others; we ignore the evidence when making some judgments but in other cases overrate what scanty evidence there is; we choose what makes us and ours feel more secure but claim to be serving the common good.[5]

Reinhold Niebuhr similarly affirmed: "The self is tempted to hide its desire to dominate the world behind its pretended devotion to the world. All mature moral conduct is therefore infected with an element of dishonesty and insincerity."[6]

Paul Tillich recognized the ambiguity of political life as the product of the historical creativity of persons. He held that the struggle between conservative and progressive forces may lead to the suppression of the creativity and validity of the opposing side. The conflicts between old and new, conserving and progressive, conservative and liberal, reach a destructive stage when either side claims ultimacy for itself.[7] When either conservative or liberal political ideologies claim to be the ultimate truth or political strategy, they become idolatrous and "demonic," according to Tillich, destructive of human and cultural well-being.

Bias, self-deception, the will to dominate others, and the ideological rigidities that produce and are supported by such are costing our society greatly in the forms of polarization, incivility, hostility, and violence that are increasingly evidenced in cultural wars. They may yet lead to something much worse and more violent. Thus, it is necessary to recognize and guard against what Konstantin Kolenda recognized as:

the tendency of human groups to freeze their standards into rigid abstractions, a persistent error which humanity has yet to learn to avoid. . . . Modern exclusivist ideologies are vestiges of . . . tribalism, precluding flexibility and compromise which would save many a person from being destroyed by the rigid demands of ideological orthodoxy. . . . The one-sidedness generated by devotion to one social ideal at the expense of another can be avoided if social ideals are evaluated in terms of their actual effect on persons.[8]

Whether or not one-sidedness can be avoided with any consistency, and whether or not it is possible that "the wisdom to know the difference" be practiced at the individual or group level in politics and church-state issues, we must all, "with understanding and compassion for all" (liberal and conservative, separationist and accommodationist) and "malice towards none" (conservative or liberal, accommodationist or separationist), affirm and embrace the wisdom of the American political system. Or, at minimum, we must be committed to tolerate the results of our democratic-republican polity as we pursue our respective political visions, philosophies, strategies, and agendas.

May we pray for and commit ourselves to the wisdom of our constitutional system and its results. Our polity and politics usually avoid the worst politically and sometimes gain the better politically. Yet, the political best—perfect justice—would seem to be beyond the grasp of any system and, certainly, of any political ideology.

Discussion Questions

1. Do you consider yourself to be a conservative or a liberal socially and politically? Why?
2. Try to understand and to appreciate the political strategy that opposes your own. Discuss the illustration of conservative and liberal political strategies on page 79. Reflect upon the answers that others gave to question 1.
3. Do you need to be more serene, accepting, and affirming of the social and political status quo than you presently are? Do you need to be more courageous, oppositional, and suspicious of the status quo than you presently are? Are you too serene (timid) and conservative or too courageous (foolhardy) and liberal in your social and political views?
4. What ulterior motives and biases do you detect in those who differ from you in your social and political views? What ulterior motives and biases can you detect in your own social and political views?
5. Discuss the need for love, at least in the minimal form of civility and respect, in our society and politics today.

Notes

[1]See James Davison Hunter, *Culture Wars: The Struggle to Define America* (Boston: Basic Books, 1991) and *Before the Shooting Starts: Searching for Democracy in America's Culture Wars* (New York: Free Press, 1994).

[2]Thomas C. Oden, *The Living God*, vol. 1 of *Systematic Theology* (New York: Harper and Row, 1987) 362.

[3]Paul Tillich, *Life and the Spirit: History and the Kingdom of God*, vol. 3 of *Systematic Theology* (Chicago: University of Chicago Press, 1963) 43.

[4]Ibid., 47.

[5]Daniel Heliminiak, *The Human Core of Spirituality: Mind as Psyche and Spirit* (Buffalo NY: State University of New York Press, 1997) 184.

[6]Reinhold Niebuhr, *Beyond Tragedy: Essays on the Christian Interpretation of History* (New York: Charles Scribner's Sons, 1937) 139.

[7]Tillich, 343-44.

[8]Konstantin Kolenda, *Cosmic Religion: The Autobiography of the Universe* (New York: Doubleday/Image Books, 1987) 88-89.

Church-State "Separation"
—the Continuing Challenge

As should be evident from the preceding essays, religious liberty issues are often far from simple in their analyses or resolutions. I recall a remark by Rabbi Samuel Karff of Houston, Texas, who ended his nuanced discussion of church-state separation with the remark: "Things are never so simple."[1] It is a remark with which I emphatically agree and that this book has sought to recognize in its analyses, arguments, and proposals. It is a perspective shared by many advocates of church-state separation and, I believe, by many who view themselves as opposed to church-state separation.

For instance, there are crucial conceptual issues that often go unacknowledged and unaddressed that make the question of the proper relations between church and state and their separation, more difficult. After all, how does one define church or religion? At one time it was the religion of Christianity or denominations of Christianity that were the primary referents of the terms. But now they refer to actions by individual Christian churches, by para-church religious and political organizations such as the Promise Keepers and the Christian Coalition, and by individual Christians acting in a governmental capacity. Church and religion may also refer to Christian religious institutions such as hospitals, private schools, and universities or to religions and religious institutions other than Christian, for example, "synagogue, temple, mosque, ashram, sangha, etc.—state separation!"

Furthermore, how do we understand the "state" in church-state separation? Originally, it meant the federal government, a government that was quite limited in its powers and presence in society. Today it means a national government in its executive, legislative, judicial, and regulatory functions that exercises broad-ranging powers and is ever-present in the public square. It also means and includes the powers of state, county, and local governments exercising similar responsibilities and powers.

And how is church-state separation to be understood and practiced? Does it entail and require a more or less absolute social/political disengagement between church and state? Due to the ubiquitous presence of government and its power in the public square, shall it result in the marginalization and banishment of religion from public life into the sphere of individual conscience and private life? First Amendment scholar Michael McConnel observes:

> When the government owns the street and parks, which are the principal sites for public communication and community celebrations, the schools, which are a principal means for transmitting ideas and values to future generations, and many of the principal institutions of culture, exclusion of religious ideas, symbols, and voices marginalizes religion in much the same way as the neglect of the contributions of African-American and other minority citizens, or of the viewpoints and contributions of women, once marginalized those segments of the society.[2]

Should church-state separation be understood to require persons of religious faith to abandon their religiously-based values in the exercise of their political rights and responsibilities as citizens, all out of concern for legislating morality or violating church-state separation?

Or should church-state separation be understood as an ideal that in practice cannot be perfectly attained or strictly maintained, and that in fact should not be advocated or attempted in an absolute and unqualified manner? Should it not denote a more nuanced, qualified, and (sometimes) compromisable autonomy and independence of both church and state, institutional religion and government, from one another? Should not whatever degree of separation of religion from government that is instituted, and whatever degree of accommodation that may be deemed necessary, be pursued for the purpose of governmental neutrality toward religion and the goal of liberty and justice for all, and not out of a hostile or dismissive attitude toward religion?

In *Zorach vs. Clauson* (1952), Justice William O. Douglas declared:

> The First Amendment . . . does not say that in every and all respects
> there shall be a separation of church and state. It studiously defines
> the manner, the specific ways, in which there shall be no concert,
> union, or dependency one upon the other. That is the common sense
> of the matter, otherwise the state and religion would be aliens to
> each other—hostile, suspicious, even unfriendly.

While it definitely was the intent of the Founding Fathers to institute
church-state separation through the Constitution, they were hardly
motivated by a general hostility, suspicion, or unfriendliness toward
religion in general!

And how shall free exercise of religion be understood? No freedom
guaranteed by the Constitution can be secured or practiced in an
absolute manner, without qualification. Freedom of religion has never
been understood, either by the Founding Fathers or by subsequent
interpreters of the Constitution, as a license for "anything goes" in the
name of religion. Free exercise also cannot mean a so-called liberty of
the majority to practice its religion in a governmentally privileged and
preferred manner in comparison to minority religions.

Some members of the Religious Right, in their calls for voluntary
public school prayer, which would actually involve governmental facil-
itation and supervision of religious expression, assume that their free
exercise can claim such governmental support and accommodation.
Free exercise cannot mean the right to a quasi-establishment that has
been, and in some localities continues to be, the case in church-state
relations.

Finally, what does non-establishment mean? For some strict separationists, any sort of governmental accommodation of religion, even
accommodation enjoyed by other nonprofit organizations within society, constitutes an establishment of religion. Anything short of a
governmental indifference, suspicion, or hostility to religion that
reflects the suspicion, hostility, and indifference toward religion held by
some militant secularists within the separationist fold, is held by some
to be an unconstitutional endorsement or aid of religion. But a policy
of governmentally-enforced religious apartheid, which such an attitude
implies, cannot be what non-establishment and church-state separation means or requires.

The preceding essays have argued that separation of church and state cannot and should not be absolute—as much or as strict as possible. Yet a robust, but properly nuanced church-state separation must be advocated, promoted, and maintained to protect both political liberty and religious liberty. Separation of church and state should be the presumption and norm with which one approaches questions of specific policies and relations between religion and government. This is due to the demonstrated perverse relations that an alliance of church and state, religion and government, has produced and may be expected to produce in the future. Past results of church-state alliances have included the diminution and destruction of liberty in general, and religious liberty in particular.

Religion—the church—will prosper when it is a free church in a free state, without preferential support of and entanglements with the state. Even if non-establishment/separationism is sometimes taken too far, and the church begins to feel that it is being "oppressed" or disfavored, the church in a very real sense continues to prosper.

But when state-church accommodation is taken too far, in conferred preferences, entanglements, and agenda-coalitions between church and state, the integrity of the state and the religious liberties of other religious persons/citizens and secularists/citizens suffers. Also, the integrity, autonomy, and free exercise of majority religion and religious institutions are threatened by excessive accommodation.

An example of such a threat may be seen in the issue of governmental vouchers to subsidize parents who wish to send their children to private religious schools. It may be the case that such a policy does not overly violate the non-establishment principle. But, as the power to tax has been recognized as the power to control and to destroy, so governmental power to fund religious institutions, even indirectly, confers the potential and inevitably very real power to control and to destroy the integrity, if not the existence, of that religious institution. What possibly may be a constitutional policy (private school vouchers) is not necessarily wise and prudential policy. Church-state separation should be valued and pursued by religion even in many of the gray areas of First Amendment questions, for it is better for the church "to be safe, than sorry" when it comes to entanglements-in-the-name-of-accommodation with government.

Furthermore, a preferentially-favored church becomes complacent, eventually spiritually indolent, and finally dictatorial and persecuting in its attempts to maintain its privileges. Incivility and civil unrest and disturbance may begin to make their appearance—and religiously motivated and rationalized incivility and civil unrest and disturbance have historically proven to be the worst kind of such phenomena.

Richard John Neuhaus recognizes that those on the Religious Right who religionize politics and politicize religion on behalf of a Christian America are doing what the Religious Left did for decades. For Neuhaus this should be a cause for worry, not for celebration. He holds that the conflation of Christian faith with a partisan political agenda inevitably leads to a distortion of faith. Moreover, such a conflation-agenda will inevitably encounter electoral setbacks, necessary compromises, and possible defeats. When the triumphalist expectations of the proponents of such a religio-political agenda are frustated, as they ultimately must be in our pluralist and democratic society, Neuhaus fears that "God and country" may produce a "God or country" mentality. The result may be "a politics aimed at dismantling what is believed to be an incorrigibly evil constitutional order."[3] Neuhaus knows, and Americans need to know, that such a perspective is alive and growing within "Reconstructionist" Christian groups today. In such circumstances, even if it succeeds in its efforts, the majority, preferentially treated religion of today may well begin to fear lest it become the minority, discriminated-against religion of tomorrow.

Michael Novak also warns those who would wish to affirm our nation as a Christian nation and also reject an energetic separation of church and state by giving governmental recognition, preferences, and privileges to Christianity and to Christians:

> Grave dangers to the human spirit lurk in the subordination of the political system and the economic system to a single moral-cultural vision. . . . An attempt to impose the Kingdom of God . . . is dangerous not only to human liberty but to Christianity itself. . . .
>
> It is particularly difficult for religious bodies to adjust to a role which removes them from command and places them outside the center. Their natural inclination is to suffuse every part of life with their own holistic vision of human nature and destiny. Since human beings are social animals . . . religious bodies properly resist being shunted aside into the private spaces of the individual heart. They

desire a public social role. Under democratic capitalism they have such a role. But it is neither in command nor at the center.

To think that they must attempt their important work only indirectly, by inspiring millions of individuals and through the competition of ideas and symbols in a pluralistic marketplace, must inevitably seem to some too demanding. Yet all this democratic capitalism asks of them.[4]

Experimenting with any alliance, entanglement, or support between church and state or departure from a basic policy of church-state separation is playing with fire; it is potentially the case, and has often been the case, that religion—the Church—gets burned! Separation of church and state as a base-line strategy, presumption, and ideal is the best fire insurance policy in the cause of religious liberty!

Notes

[1]Houston Chapter of Americans United for Separation of Church and State, October 1996, Houston TX.

[2]Michael McConnel, quoted in Warren Nord, *Religion and American Education: Rethinking a National Dilemma* (Chapel Hill NC: University of North Carolina Press, 1995) 130.

[3]Richard John Neuhaus, "Against Christian Politics," *First Things* (May 1996): 73.

[4]Michael Novak, *The Spirit of Democratic Capitalism* (New York: Simon and Schuster/Touchstone Books, 1983) 68-69. For a further development of this view, see Novak's masterful *Free Persons and the Common Good* (Lanham MD: Madison Books, 1989).

The United States Constitution (Excerpts)

Preamble

We, the people of the United States, in Order to form a more perfect Union, establish justice, insure domestic Tranquility, provide for the common defence, promote the general Welfare, and secure the Blessings of Liberty to ourselves and our Posterity, do ordain and establish this Constitution for the United States of America.

> [Note, the Preamble nowhere appeals to divine or biblical authority or to Christian purposes. "The people" are the authority. A more perfect union, the establishment of justice, the insurance of domestic tranquility, provision for the common "defence," the promotion of the general welfare, and securing the blessings of liberty are the purposes for which the Constitution was created. The Founding Fathers tell us in this preamble what they were seeking to accomplish—and it should be obvious that they were not concerned to accomplish what they did not state as their purpose in the Preamble.]*

First Amendment

Congress shall make no law respecting an establishment of religion, or prohibiting the free exercise thereof; or abridging the freedom of speech, or of the press, or the right of the people peaceably to assemble, and to petition the Government for a redress of grievances.

> [Congress is prohibited to make *any* law "respecting" an establishment of religion. The prohibition is not merely addressed to *some* laws officially establishing religion, but to *any* law "respecting" (concerning) an establishment of religion. Moreover, it is "religion"

*[In all appendices, author's notes appear in brackets.]

—not "a religion" or a "sect" of religion, as the Founding Fathers often referred to particular churches and denominations —that may not be established or prohibited free exercise. In addition, "or prohibiting the free exercise thereof" is the second religious liberty clause and the second clause in the First Amendment, as "or abridging the freedom of speech" is the third, "or of the press" is the fourth clause, and so on. It is unfortunately necessary to emphasize that the First Amendment is now properly applied to the states also.]

Ninth Amendment

The enumeration in the Constitution, of certain rights, shall not be construed to deny or disparage others retained by the people.

[The Ninth Amendment is a reminder that the Constitution does not create or confer rights. It recognizes and "secures" natural rights. Just because a right is not mentioned or "enumerated" in the text of the Constitution does not mean that no such right exists or that it is inferior to those enumerated. There are rights other than those named in the Bill of Rights that humans possess by nature and as a divine endowment. Upon their public claim and recognition, government is also bound to secure these rights.]

Fourteenth Amendment

Section 1. All persons born or naturalized in the United States, and subject to the jurisdiction thereof, are citizens of the United States and of the State wherein they reside. No state shall make or enforce any law which shall abridge the privileges or immunities of citizens of the United States, nor shall any State deprive any person of life, liberty, or property, without due process of law; nor deny to any person within its jurisdiction the equal protection of the laws.

[The Civil War and the Fourteenth Amendment settled the issue of national supremacy over state sovereignty. National citizenship is primary, and state citizenship is not a matter of state sovereignty, but of Constitutional dictate. The "privileges and immunities" of national citizenship must not be abridged by state action. (Contra the 5 to 4 split decision by the Supreme Court in the "Slaughterhouse Cases.") Nor may states deny their citizens "equal protection of the (state) laws." And there is no textual or historical justification for limiting the reference of this amendment to African-Americans only.]

A Bill for Establishing Religious Freedom (Excerpts)

[This religious freedom bill was proposed by Thomas Jefferson to the Virginia Assembly in 1779 and adopted, as a result of the vigorous promotion of the bill by James Madison, in 1785.]

Well aware that the opinions and belief of men depend not upon their own will, but follow involuntarily the evidence proposed to their own minds, that Almighty God hath created the mind free, and manifested his supreme will that free it shall remain by making it altogether insusceptible of restraint, that all attempts to influence it by temporal punishments, or burthens, or by civil incapacitations, tend only to beget habits of hypocrisy and meanness, and are a departure from the plan of the holy author of our religion, who being lord of both body and mind, yet chose not to propagate it by coercions on either, as was in his Almighty power to do, but to extend it by its influence on reason alone; that the impious presumption of legislators and rulers, civil as well as ecclesiastical, who, being themselves but fallible and uninspired men, have assumed dominion over the faith of others, setting up their own opinions and modes of thinking as the only true and infallible, and as such endeavoring to impose them on others, hath established and maintained false religions over the greatest part of the world and through all time: . . . that our civil rights have no dependence upon our religious opinions, any more than our opinions in physics or geometry; that therefore the proscribing any citizen as unworthy the public confidence by laying upon him an incapacity of being called to offices of trust and emolument, unless he profess or renounce this or that religious opinion, is depriving him injuriously of those privileges and advantages to which, in common with his fellow citizens he has a natural right, that it tends also to corrupt the principles of that very religion it is meant to encourage, by bribing, with a monopoly of worldly honours and emoluments, those who will externally confess and conform to it; . . . that the opinions of men are not the object of civil government, nor under its jurisdiction; . . .

We, the General Assembly of Virginia do enact that no man shall be compelled to frequent or support any religious worship, place, or ministry whatsoever, nor shall be enforced, restrained, molested, or burthened in his body or goods, nor shall otherwise suffer, on account of his religious opinions or belief; but that all men shall be free to profess, and by arguments to maintain, their opinions in matters of religion, and that the same shall in no wise diminish, enlarge, or affect their civil capacities.

. . . We . . . declare, that the rights hereby asserted are of the natural rights of mankind, and that if any [legislative] act shall be hereafter passed to repeal the present [legislation] or to narrow its operation, such an act will be an infringement of natural right. . . .

A Memorial and Remonstrance Against Religious Assessments (Excerpts)

[James Madison wrote this Memorial in 1785 in opposition to a proposal to the Virginia House of Delegates to provide state financial aid, in the form of assessments, for the teaching of religion. The bill, a "nonpreferentialist" proposal for state aid to religion advocated by Patrick Henry, was subsequently defeated. Note that Madison equates nonpreferential aid to Christian religious teaching as "establishment" of religion.]

. . . We remonstrate against the said Bill,

1. Because we hold it for a fundamental and undeniable truth, "that Religion or the duty we owe to our Creator and the manner of discharging it, can be directed only by reason and conviction, not by force or violence." The Religion then of every man must be left to the conviction and conscience of every man; and it is the right of every man to exercise it as these may dictate. The right is in its nature an unalienable right. . . . We maintain therefore that in matters of Religion, no man's right is abridged by the institution of Civil Society and that Religion is wholly exempt from its cognizance.

4. Because the Bill violates that equality which ought to be the basis of every law . . . If "all men are by nature equally free and independent," all men are to be considered as entering into Society on equal conditions; as relinquishing no more, and therefore retaining no less, one than another, of their natural rights. Above all are they to be considered as retaining " an equal title to the free exercise of religion according to the dictates of conscience." Whilst we assert for ourselves a freedom to embrace, to profess and to observe the Religion which we believe to be of divine origin, we cannot deny an equal freedom to

those whose minds have not yet yielded to the evidence which has convinced us. If this freedom be abused, it is an offence against God, not against man: To God, therefore, not to man, must an account of it be rendered. As the Bill violates equality by subjecting some to particular burdens, so it violates the same principle, by granting to others peculiar exemptions.

8. Because the establishment in question is not necessary for the support of the Civil Government. . . . If religion be not within the cognizance of Civil Government how can its legal establishment be necessary to Civil Government? What influence in fact have ecclesiastical establishments had on Civil Society? In some instances they have been seen to erect a spiritual tyranny on the ruins of the Civil authority; in many instances they have been seen upholding the thrones of political tyranny: in no instance have they been seen the guardians of the liberties of the people. Rulers who wish to subvert the public liberty, may have found an established Clergy convenient auxiliaries. A just government instituted to secure & perpetuate it needs them not. Such a Government will best be supported by protecting every Citizen in the enjoyment of his Religion with the same equal hand which protects his person and his property; by neither invading the equal rights of any Sect, nor suffering any Sect to invade those of another.

11. Because it will destroy that moderation and harmony which the forbearance of our laws to intermeddle with Religion has produced among its several sects. . . .

12. Because finally, "the equal right of every citizen to the free exercise of his Religion according to the dictates of conscience" is held by the same tenure with all our other rights. If we recur to its origin, it is equally the gift of nature; if we weigh its importance, it cannot be less dear to us; . . . Either then, we must say, that the Will of the Legislature is the only measure of their authority; and that in the plenitude of this authority, they may sweep away all our fundamental rights; or, that they are bound to leave this particular right untouched and sacred: . . .

Thomas Jefferson's Letter to the Danbury Baptist Association (Excerpts)

January 1, 1802

Gentlemen:

The affectionate sentiments of esteem and appreciation which you are so good to express toward me, on behalf of the Danbury Baptist Association, give me the highest satisfaction. My duties dictate a faithful and zealous pursuit of the interests of my constituents, and in proportion as they are persuaded of my fidelity to those duties, the discharge of them becomes more and more pleasing.

Believing with you that religion is a matter that lies solely between man and his God, and that he owes to none other for his faith or his worship, that the legislative powers of government reach actions only, and not opinions, I contemplate with sovereign reverence that act of the whole American people which declared that their legislature should "make no law respecting an establishment of religion, or prohibiting the free exercise thereof," thus building a wall of separation between church and state.

Adhering to this supreme expression of the will of the Nation in behalf of rights of conscience, I shall see with sincere satisfaction the progress of those sentiments which tend to restore to man his natural rights, convinced he has no natural right in opposition to his social duties.

I reciprocate your kind prayers for the protection and blessing of the Common Father and Creator of man, and tender you for yourselves and your religious association, assurances of high respect and esteem.

—*Thomas Jefferson*

Americans United Manifesto "To Repair the Breach" (Excerpts)

. . . Americans United does not concern itself with the religious teaching, the forms of worship, or the ecclesiastical organization of the many churches in our country. It is no part of our purpose to propagandize the Protestant faith or any other, nor to criticize the teachings or internal practices of the Roman Catholic Church or any other. We have no connection or sympathy with any movement that is tinged with religious fanaticism. Our motivation arises solely from our patriotic and religious concern for the maintenance of the separation of church and state under the American form of government.

. . . Congress and all State legislatures, and all executive and judiciary agencies of government must be warned that they are playing with fire when they play into the hands of any church which seeks at any point, however marginal, to breach the wall that sharply separates church and state in this country. The principle of their separation is so firmly established in a long tradition as well as in the Constitution that any tampering with it will tend to light the fires of intolerance and fanaticism which our system of government is designed to prevent.

. . . Americans United has come into existence to defend this open forum of religious liberty against its violation by law or the administration of law. The state is forbidden to invade this area. It may not by law or administration of law accord to any church a status which gives it a special advantage in the wide domain of religious freedom. This is the plain meaning of the first Amendment, which forbids Congress to make any law "respecting an establishment of religion"—that is, pertaining to, or leading toward, such an establishment.

. . . The Federal Supreme Court in two decisions has confirmed State legislation which sanctions the use of public school funds to provide free textbooks for parochial schools (1930) [*Cochran vs. Board of Education*] and to transport pupils to such schools (1947) [*Everson vs. Board of Education*]. The four dissenting justices in the bus-transportation case solemnly warned the nation that these two breaches in the wall separating church and state are only the beginning. "That a third and fourth breach, and still others, will be attempted, we may be sure," say the dissenting justices.

. . . Americans United is determined to assert its full strength to the end that there shall be no more breaches in this wall, that the breaches already made shall be repaired, and that the complete separation of church and state in an undivided state-supported educational system shall be maintained.

. . . Americans United proposes to carry on a campaign of Enlightenment and mobilization of public opinion throughout the nation until the vital issue which has been raised by these violations and the threat of further violations has been decided by the voice of the people.

The Americanism of the people's representatives in the various branches of the government must be stiffened against the promptings of sentimentalism or the low dictates of political advantage to resist the aggressive activities of those who would subvert the Constitution to their own sectarian interest. . . .

Twelve Rules for Mixing Religion and Politics (Excerpts)

[*Twelve Rules for Mixing Religion and Politics* is based on a 1984 People for the American Way publication by Jim Castelli. This 1994 edition was written by Matthew Freeman, Director of Research and Program Development. It is reproduced here by the kind permission of People for the American Way.]

Introduction

The proper relationship between church and state has long been a source of controversy. Throughout American history, government has grappled with the challenge of protecting religious liberty without "establishing" religion, while religious institutions have time and time again examined their role in public policy formation. . . .

Increasingly, religion and religious views are becoming a part of political debate in America, and the media prism through which most Americans receive their information seems to distort the very complex issues into simplistic images. The result is a process ripe for exploitation by demagogues from both ends of the debate.

Whenever religious issues are introduced into the political dialogue, criticism inevitable arises that various players are inappropriately mixing religion and politics, something these critics maintain violates the constitutional separation of church and state. The truth is that religion and politics are appropriately mixed all the time—whenever political players cite their personal religious views as a factor in their stand on issues, or when like-minded members of a church, synagogue or mosque organize for political ends, to name just two examples. Such activities are not in and of themselves violations of the constitutional separation of church and state. After all, the Constitution and Bill of Rights speak to the boundaries between the *institutions* of church and state, not to the looser mixing of religious and political dialogue or thought. In the end, it is virtually impossible *not* to mix religion and politics to some degree. After all, the same values that shape political beliefs shape religious beliefs.

For the same reason, it is also unwise to separate religious beliefs from the political process altogether. After all, morality—for most Americans a concept inextricably woven with their religious views—undergirds any system of law and justice. It provides a compass that enables many Americans to navigate the difficult waters of increasingly complex issues. . . .

As we address the various challenges confronting our nation, it's particularly important that Americans find the proper mix [between religion and politics]. The American system of religious pluralism is unique; it developed largely because people fled lands where the mix was improper—where religious dissent and diversity were not respected. But the same founding generation that took such pains to preserve our religious freedom also brought religious values to bear in shaping their new land. Those values continue to undergird many Americans' understanding of their communities and their nation, and the contributions those religious values make to American culture and government are mighty indeed. Sadly, as long as some persist in wielding religion as a political club, any and all religious expression in the public square seems to generate criticism from some quarter.

It is important then to establish consensual guidelines for how best to mix religion and politics—not just to protect against inappropriate mixing, but to encourage religious voices from the hundreds of active religions in America to join the debate over public-policy matters, free from fears of attacks on their right to take part.

Government and Religion

The following address the appropriate role of religion and religious views in the policy-making process.

Rule One:
Religious doctrine alone is not an acceptable basis for government policy.

Because government represents all the people, not just those whose faiths are consistent with those of government officials, it is inappropriate for government policy to be based solely on religious doctrine. Such doctrine is acceptable only to those who share a particular faith, and it is not open to reasonable debate in the way that public policy positions are. . . .

Of course, while government institutions hold no particular religious view, individual government officials and unelected players in the political process plainly do. They must not be expected to abandon their faith as a price for taking part in the process. They are and should be free to espouse their religious views, and to discuss the role those views lay in their thinking on a given issue. That said, they must understand that not all Americans share their particular faith, and will therefore not necessarily find their arguments compelling.

Moreover, they cannot expect the government to accept their religious arguments as a determining factor in a public policy decision-making. To do so would be to base public policy solely upon theology, a lain violation of church-state separation. Indeed, when advocates rely solely on religious grounds to make their case, they run the risk, should they succeed, that the courts will find that government officials acted for religious purposes—a likely church-state violation.

Rule Two:
There can be no religious test for public office, nor religious test for participating in the political process. . . .

Rule Three:
Public officials have every right to express their private piety, and no right at all to use their office to proselytize others. . . .

To be sure, Americans are accustomed to a certain measure of piety in their public officials, and national leaders frequently call for God's help or blessing in times of crisis. These sorts of non-denominational references to public officials' private faith are wholly appropriate, and Americans do not find them threatening or disturbing. But a public official who asks people to believe in the Bible, or to do something because it is commanded by "Our Lord, Jesus Christ" has stepped out of bounds.

Church and State

The following speak to the appropriate relationship between the institutions of church and state.

Rule Four:
Government has a right to demand that religious institutions comply with reasonable regulation and social policy.

The Constitution provides that while government must be neutral toward religion, it must also accommodate it. However, that accommodation does not provide religious institutions *carte blanche* to ignore reasonable government regulation. . . .

Where the question of government regulation has been most in dispute in recent years has been over the question of taxation of the political activity of churches or other institutions that claim religious exemption. . . .

Electoral politics . . . is not a tax-free activity. Contributions to religious candidates are not tax-deductible and organizations that work to elect candidates are not tax-exempt. So when religious institutions engage in such activities, they exceed the bounds of what they are permitted to do under benefit of tax exemption. The institutions are free to engage in such behavior, but they may not continue to operate as a tax-exempt organization. . . .

Rule Five:
Religious institutions may sometimes cooperate with government in programs supporting the common good.

The absolutist approach to church-state separation would bar any and al cooperation between government and religious institutions. But this approach ignores the practical reality that most churches engage in a variety of charitable activities that are not specifically religious in nature. For example, religious institutions are vital partners in the effort to house the homeless and feed the hungry. Indeed, over the years, churches, synagogues, and other religious institutions have been able partners with government in disaster relief efforts, diagnostic health testing campaigns and more. Such efforts are perfectly appropriate and vitally needed.

Still the area is a murky one. . . . Very generally, the government should not be in the business of promoting or subsidizing the transmission of religious beliefs. To the extent that such cooperation between religious institutions and government involves the transmission of such beliefs, the cooperation is inappropriate and constitutes an establishment of religion. . . .

Rule Six:
Government institutions must show neither official approval or disapproval of religion.

. . . The principle of government neutrality toward religion speaks not just to favoritism among different religions, but to a preference for religion as opposed to irreligion. Although the vast majority of Americans profess a belief in God and a similar majority affiliate themselves with one of the hundreds of active religions in the land, our secular government holds no official religious view and should not seek to promote one. . . .

Religion and Religious Views in the Public Square

The following addresses the ways in which individuals and political leaders employ religious doctrine and rhetoric in the political dialogue.

Rule Seven:
Political discourse should respect religious differences.

As important as it is to respect religious values in the political debate, it is equally important to respect religious differences. . . .

Over the years, various political figures have denigrated minority religions or religious views as a way to marginalize their political opposition. For example, leaders of some organizations routinely accuse their opponents of representing "New Age" philosophy. . . . Do the adherents of New Age views have a somehow diminished right to participation in the political process? And is it appropriate to belittle their religious views as a means to a political end?

The same criticism could be made of those who belittle the views of fundamentalist Christians as a way to advance their own political agenda. . . . The religious views that drive those political views are deserving of respect.

In the context of this rule, it is especially important that participants in the political process not make assumptions about the religious views of others. Some political figures' rhetoric dismisses the views of others as being the result of atheism, or anti-Christian bigotry. Such rhetoric is rarely supported by fact, and casts a ugly cloud over the debate. . . .

Cardinal Joseph Bernardin put it this way: "We should maintain and clearly articulate our religious convictions, but also maintain our civil courtesy. We should be vigorous in stating a case and attentive in hearing another's case; we should test everyone's logic, but not question his or her motives."

Rule Eight:
Political figures should not claim to represent a monolithic religious constituency, and the media and others should not attribute such a constituency to them.

. . . Christians belong to a wide variety of denominations and subscribe to an even broader array of political opinions. For that reason, it is unfair for any political or religious figure to claim to speak for all Christians, or to otherwise suggest that their view is representative of Christians. Not only does it stretch these leaders' constituency far beyond what they can fairly claim, and not only does it effectively disenfranchise those constituents who do not share the expressed religious views, it does something else much more troubling: it suggests that those who do not share the particular political views are unworthy of describing themselves as Christians. . . .

Rule Nine:
It is appropriate to discuss the moral dimension of public issues.

In their haste to dismiss the arguments of the Religious Right, many critics charge that the movement seeks to legislate its own morality. This argument often carries with it the suggestion that morality has no place in public policy debate. Not only does such a view ignore the plain moral dimension of many issues, it makes for bad policy. . . .

Syndicated columnist George Will spoke to the distinction between religious doctrine and morality in a mid-1980s column. Chastising the Religious Right, he wrote: "American politics is currently afflicted by kinds of grim, moralizing groups that are course in their conceptions, vulgar in analysis and intemperate in advocacy. But the desirable alternative to such groups is not less preoccupation with this sort of question, but better preoccupation. . . . Absent good moral argument, bad moral argument will have the field to itself.

Rule Ten:
Political discussion of morality is best applied to the common good, not to private conduct.

This is a time-worn principle that has come under recent attack, but it makes good sense for several reasons. First, consensus is more readily achievable on public policy issues than on matters of private action . . .

A second problem with political debate over private morality is that government cannot effectively enforce private morality that has no public manifestation. Indeed, efforts to do so generally end up weakening respect for law . . .

Overemphasis on private morality can obscure the responsibility of religion and morality in protecting the common good. . . .

Rule Eleven:
No one should claim or suggest that they speak for God on matters of public policy.

. . . Statements that claim or suggest God's endorsement are protected by the First Amendment to the Constitution. But that does not make them a constructive addition to the political or theological dialogue.

Rule Twelve:
Religion should not be used as a political club.

. . . Americans have always found in their worship the lessons of charity, faith, hope, love and community. Those in our political process who seek to use religion to divide Americans from one another, or to create a hierarchy of faith for political purposes do violence not just to the political process, but to the institution of religion as well.

The Williamsburg Charter
(Excerpts)

Keenly aware of the high national purpose of commemorating the bicentennial of the United States Constitution, we who sign this Charter seek to celebrate the Constitution's greatness, and to call for a bold reaffirmation and reappraisal of its vision and guiding principles. In particular, we call for a fresh consideration of religious liberty in our time, and of the place of the First Amendment Religious Liberty clauses in our national life.

. . . In spite of its enduring and universal qualities . . . some provisions of the Constitution are now the subject of widespread controversy in the United States. One area of intense controversy concerns the First Amendment Religious Liberty clauses, whose mutually reinforcing provisions act as a double guarantee of religious liberty, one part barring the making of any law "respecting an establishment of religion" and the other barring any law "prohibiting the free exercise thereof."

. . . We judge that the present controversies over religion in public life pose both a danger and an opportunity. There is evident danger in the fact that certain forms of politically reassertive religion in parts of the world are, in principle, enemies of democratic freedom and a source of deep social antagonism. There is also evident opportunity in their growing philosophical and cultural awareness that all people live by commitments and ideals, and value-neutrality is impossible in the ordering of society, and that we are on the edge of a promising moment for a fresh assessment of pluralism and liberty. It is with an eye to both the promise and the peril that we publish this Charter and pledge ourselves to its principles.

A Time for Reaffirmation

. . . We believe, in the first place, that the nature of the Religious Liberty clauses must be understood before the problems surrounding them can be resolved. We therefore affirm both their cardinal assumptions and the reasons for their crucial national importance.

With regard to the assumptions of the First Amendment Religious Liberty clauses, we hold three to be chief:

The Inalienable Right

. . . As James Madison expressed in his Memorial and remonstrance, "The religion of every man must be left to the conviction and conscience of every man; and it is the right of every man to exercise it as these may dictate. This right is in its nature an inalienable right."

. . . Religious liberty finally depends on neither the favors of the state and its officials nor the vagaries of tyrants or majorities. Religious liberty in a democracy is a right that may not be submitted to vote and depends upon the outcome of no election. A society is only as just and free as it is respectful of this right, especially towards the beliefs of its smallest minorities and least popular communities.

The right to freedom of conscience is premised not upon science, nor upon social utility, nor upon pride of species. Rather, it is premised upon the inviolable dignity of the human person. It is the foundation of, and is integrally related to, all other rights and freedoms secured by the Constitution. . . .

The Ever Present Danger

No threat to freedom of conscience and religious liberty has historically been greater than the coercions of both Church and State. These two institutions—the one religious, the other political—have through the centuries succumbed to the temptation of coercion in their claims over minds and souls. When these institutions and their claims have been combined, it has too often resulted in terrible violations of human liberty and dignity. They are so combined when the sword and the purse of the State are in the hands of the church, or when the State usurps the mantle of the Church so as to coerce the conscience and compel belief. These and other confusions of religion and state authority represent the misordering of religion and government which it is the purpose of the Religious Liberty provisions to prevent.

. . .Whether ancient or modern, issuing from religion or ideology, the result is the same: religious and ideological orthodoxies, when politically established, lead only too naturally toward what Roger Williams called a "spiritual rape" that coerces the conscience and produces "rivers of civil blood" that stain the record of human history.

Less dramatic but also lethal to freedom and the chief menace to religious liberty today is the expanding power of government control over personal behavior and the institutions of society, when the government acts not so much in deliberate hostility to, but in reckless disregard of, communal belief and personal conscience. . . .

The Most Nearly Perfect Solution

Knowing well that "nothing human can be perfect" (James Madison) and that the Constitution was not "a faultless work" (Gouverneur Morris), the Framers nevertheless saw the First Amendment as a "true remedy" and the most nearly perfect solution yet devised for properly ordering the relationship of religion and the state in a free society.

There have been occasions when the protections of the First Amendment have been overridden or imperfectly applied. . . . limitation upon religious liberty is allowable only where the State has borne a heavy burden of proof that the limitation is justified—not by any ordinary public interest, but by a supreme public necessity—and that no less restrictive alternative to limitation exists.

The Religious Liberty clauses are a brilliant construct in which both No establishment and Free Exercise serve the ends of religious liberty and freedom of conscience. . . . Now, the government is barred from using religion's mantle to become a confessional State, and from allowing religion to use the government's sword and purse to become a coercing Church. In this new order, the freedom of government from religious control and the freedom of religion from government control are a double guarantee of the protection of rights. No faith is preferred or prohibited, for where there is no state-definable orthodoxy, there can be no state-punishable heresy.

With regard to the reasons why the First Amendment Religious Liberty clauses are important for the nation today, we hold five to be preeminent:

The First Amendment Religious Liberty provisions have both a logical and a historical priority in the Bill of Rights.

. . .The First Amendment Religious Liberty provisions lie close to the heart of the distinctiveness of the American experiment.

. . .The First Amendment Religious Liberty provisions are the democratic world's most salient alternative to the totalitarian repression of human right and provide a corrective to unbridled nationalism and religious warfare around the world.

. . .The First Amendment Religious Liberty provisions provide the United States' most distinctive answer to one of the world's most pressing questions in the late twentieth century. They address the problem: How do we live with each others' differences?

. . .The First Amendment Religious Liberty provisions give American society a unique position in relation to both First and Third worlds. Highly modernized like the rest of the First World, yet not so secularized, this society—largely because of religious freedom—remains, like most of the Third World, deeply religious. This fact . . . is critical for possibilities of better human understanding . . .

In sum, as much if not more than any other single provision in the entire Constitution, the Religious Liberty provisions hold the key to American distinctiveness and American destiny. Far from being settled by the interpretations of judges and historians, the last word on the first Amendment likely rests in a chapter yet to be written, documenting the unfolding drama of America. If religious liberty is neglected. All civil liberties will suffer. If it is guarded and sustained, the American experiment will be the more secure.

A Time for Reappraisal

Much of the current controversy about religion and politics neither reflects the highest wisdom of the First Amendment nor serves the best interests of the nation. We therefore call for a critical reappraisal of the course and consequences of such controversy. Four widespread errors have exacerbated the controversy needlessly.

The Issue Is Not Only What We Debate, But How

The debate about religion in public life is too often misconstrued as a clash of ideologies alone, pitting "secularists" against the "sectarians" or vice versa. Though competing and even contrary worldviews

112

are involved, the controversy is not solely ideological. It also flows from a breakdown in understanding of how personal and communal beliefs should be related to public life.

The American republic depends upon the answers to two questions. By what ultimate truths ought we to live? And how should these be related to public life? The first question is personal, but has a public dimension because of the connection between beliefs and public virtue. The American answer to the first question is that the government is excluded from giving an answer. The second question, however, is thoroughly public in character, and a public answer is appropriate and necessary to the well-being of this society.

This second question was central to the idea of the First Amendment. The Religious Liberty provisions are not "articles of faith" concerned with the substance of particular doctrines or of policy issues. They are "articles of peace" concerned with the constitutional constraints and the shared prior understanding within which the American people can engage their differences in a civil manner and thus provide for both religious liberty and stable public governments.

Conflicts over the relationship between deeply held beliefs and public policy will remain a continuing feature of democratic life. They do not discredit the First Amendment, but confirm its wisdom and point to the need to distinguish the Religious Liberty clauses from the particular controversies they address. . . .

The Issue Is Not Sectarian, But National

The role of religion in American public life is too often devalued or dismissed in public debate, as though the American people's historically vital religious traditions were at best a purely private matter and at worst sectarian and divisive.

Such a position betrays a failure of civil respect for the convictions of others. It also underestimates the degree to which the Framers relied on the American people's religious convictions to be what Tocqueville described as "the first of their political institutions." In America, this crucial public role has been played by diverse beliefs, not so much despite disestablishment as because of disestablishment. . . .

The Issue Is Larger Than the Disputants

Recent controversies over religion and public life have too often become a form of warfare in which individuals, motives and reputations have been impugned. The intensity of the debate is commensurate with the importance of the issues declared, but to those engaged in this warfare we present two arguments for reappraisal and restraint.

The lesser argument is one of expediency and is based on the ironic fact that each side has become the best argument for the other. One side's excesses have become the other side's arguments; one side's extremists the other's recruiters. The danger is that, as the ideological warfare becomes self-perpetuating, more serious issues and broader national interests will be forgotten and the bitterness deepened.

The more important question is one of principle and is based on the fact that the several sides have pursued their objectives in ways which contradict their own best ideals. Too often, for example, religious believer's have been uncharitable, liberals have been illiberal, conservatives have been insensitive to tradition, champions of tolerance have been intolerant, defenders of free speech have been censorious, and citizens of a republic based upon democratic accommodation have succumbed to a habit of relentless confrontation.

The Issue Is Understandably Threatening

The First Amendment's meaning is too often debated in ways that ignore the genuine grievances or justifiable fears of opposing points of view. This happens when the logic of opposing arguments favors either an unwarranted intrusion of religion into public life or a unwarranted exclusion of religion from it. History plainly shows that with religious control over government, political freedom dies; with political control over religion, religious freedom dies.

. . . In earlier times, though lasting well into the twentieth century, there was a *de facto* semi-establishment of one religion in the United States: a generalized Protestantism given dominant national status in national institutions, especially in the public schools. . . .

In more recent times, and partly in reaction, constitutional jurisprudence has tended, in the view of many, to move toward a *de facto* semi-establishment of a wholly sectarian understanding of the origin, nature and destiny of humankind and of the American nation. During this period, the exclusion of teaching about the role of religion in society, based partly upon a misunderstanding of First Amendment decisions, has ironically resulted in giving a dominant status to such wholly secular understandings in many national institutions. Many secularists appear as unconcerned over the consequences of this development as were Protestants unconcerned about their *de facto* establishment earlier.

Such *de facto* establishments, though seldom extreme, usually benign and often unwitting, are the source of grievances and fears among the several parties in the current controversies. . . .

Justifiable fears are raised by those who advocate theocracy or the coercive power of law to establish a "Christian America." . . .

At the same time there are others who raise justifiable fears of a unwarranted exclusion of religion from public life. . . .

Two important conclusions follow from a reappraisal of the present controversies over religion in public life. First, the process of adjustment and readjustment to the constraints and standards of the Religious Liberty provisions is an ongoing requirement of American democracy. The Constitution is not a self-interpreting, self-executing document; and the prescriptions of the Religious Liberty provisions cannot by themselves resolve the myriad confusions and ambiguities surrounding the right ordering of the relationship between religion and government in a free society. The Framers clearly understood that the Religious Liberty provisions provide the legal construct for what must be an ongoing process of adjustment and mutual give-and-take in a democracy.

. . .Thus, we cannot have, and should not seek, a definitive, once for all solution to the questions that will continue to surround the Religious Liberty provisions.

Second, the need for such a readjustment today can best be addressed by remembering that the two clauses are essentially one provision for preserving religious liberty. Both parts, No-Establishment and Free Exercise, are to be comprehensively understood as being in the service of religious liberty as a positive good. . . .

A Time for Reconstitution

We believe, finally, that the time is ripe for a genuine expansion of democratic liberty, and that this goal may be attained through a new engagement of citizens that is reordered in accord with the constitu-tional first principles and consideration of the common good. . . . Careful consideration of three precepts would advance this possibility.

The Criteria Must Be Multiple

Reconstitution requires the recognition that the great dangers in interpreting the Constitution today are either to release interpretation from any demanding criteria or to narrow the criteria excessively. The first relaxes the restraining force of the Constitution, while the second overlooks the insights that have arisen from the Constitution in two centuries of national experience.

. . .The Religious Liberty provisions must be understood both in terms of the Framers' intentions and history's sometimes surprising results. Interpreting and applying them today requires not only histori-cal research but moral and political reflection.

The intention of the Framers is therefore a necessary but insuffi-cient criterion for interpreting and applying the Constitution. . . . We must take the purpose and text of the Constitution seriously, sustain the principles behind the words and add an appreciation of the many-sided genius of the First Amendment and its complex development over time.

The Consensus Must Be Dynamic

. . . Religious liberty is indisputably what the Framers intended and what the First Amendment has preserved. Far from being a matter of exemption, exception or even toleration, religious liberty is an inalien-able right. Far from being a sub-category of free speech or a constitu-tional redundancy, religious liberty is distinct and foundational. Far from being simply an individual right, religious liberty is a positive social good.

. . . In light of the First Amendment, the government should stand in relation to the churches, synagogues and other communities of faith as a guarantor of freedom. In light of the First Amendment, the churches, synagogues and other communities of faith stand in relation to the government as generators of faith, and therefore contribute to the spiritual and moral foundations of democracy. Thus, the govern-ment acts as a safeguard, but not the source, of freedom for faiths, whereas the churches and synagogues act as a source, but not the safeguard, of faiths for freedom.

. . . Neither established nor excluded, neither preferred nor proscribed, each faith (whether transcendent or naturalistic) is brought into a relationship with the government so that each is separated from the state in terms of its institutions, but democratically related to the state in terms of its individuals and its ideas.

The result is neither a naked public square where all religion is excluded, nor a sacred public square with any religion established or semi-established. The result, rather, is a civil public square in which the citizens of all religious faiths, or none, engage one another in the continuing public discourse.

The Compact Must Be Mutual

. . .That rights are universal and responsibilities are mutual is both the premise and the promise of democratic pluralism. The First Amendment, in this sense, is the epitome of public justice and serves as the golden rule for civic life. Rights are best guarded and responsibilities best exercised when each and person and groups guards for all others those rights they wish for themselves. . . .

From this axiom, that rights are universal and responsibilities mutual, derives guidelines for conducting public debates involving religion in a manner that is democratic and civil. These guidelines are not, and must not be, mandated by law. But they are, we believe, necessary to reconstitute and revitalize the American understanding of the rule of religion in a free society.

First, those who claim the right to dissent should assume the responsibility to debate. . . .

Second, those who claim the right to criticize should assume the responsibility to comprehend.

. . .The right to argue for any public policy is a fundamental right for every citizen; respecting that right is a fundamental responsibility for all other citizens. When any view is expressed, all must uphold as constitutionally protected its advocate's right to express it. But others are free to challenge that view as politically pernicious, philosophically false, ethically evil, theologically idolatrous, or simply absurd, as the case may seem to be.

. . .Third, those who claim the right to influence should respect the responsibility not to inflame: Too often in recent disputes over religion and public affairs, some have insisted that any evidence of religious influence on public policy represents an establishment of religion and is therefore precluded as an improper "imposition." Such exclusion of religion from public life is historically unwarranted, philosophically inconsistent and profoundly undemocratic. . . .

Religious liberty and democratic civility are also threatened, however, from another quarter. Overreacting to an improper veto on religion in public life, many have used religious language and images not for the legitimate influencing of politics but to inflame politics. . . . Some err by refusing to recognize that there is a distinction, though not a separation, between religion and politics. As a result, they bring to politics a misplaced absoluteness that idolizes politics, "Satanizes" their enemies and politicizes their own faith.

. . .Fourth, those who claim the right to participate should accept the responsibility to persuade: Central to the American experience is the power of political persuasion. Growing partly from principle and partly from the pressures of democratic pluralism, commitment to persuasion is the corollary of the belief that conscience is inviolable, coercion of the conscience is evil, and the public interest is best served by consent hard won by vigorous debate. . . . To those who subscribe to the idea of government by the consent of the governed, compelled beliefs are a violation of first principles. The natural logic of the Religious Liberty provisions is to foster a political culture of persuasion which admits the challenge of opinions from all sources.

Arguments for public policy should be more than private convictions shouted out loud. For persuasion to be principled, private convictions should be translated into publicly accessible claims. . . .

Renewal of First Principles

. . .We address ourselves to our fellow citizens, daring to hope that the strongest desire of the greatest number is for the common good. We are firmly persuaded that the principles asserted here require a fresh consideration, and that the renewal of religious liberty is crucial to sustain a free people that would remain free. We therefore commit ourselves to speak, write and act according to this vision and these principles. We urge our fellow citizens to do the same. . . .

The Ten Commandments of Moderate Political Behavior (Excerpts)

[Chapter 5 of *How Right Is the Right?: A Biblical and Balanced Approach to Politics*, "The Ten Commandments of Moderate Political Behavior," is termed the centerpiece of the work by authors Randall L. Frame and Alan Tharpe. Following are their words:]

This chapter consists of ten clearly stated principles that, if applied, would go a long way toward loosening the chains of ideological captivation without compromising th moral voice the church must uphold to the world. These commandments presume that, particularly when it comes to matters of public policy, sincere, intelligent people—including Christian people—can and do disagree. They also presume that Christian citizens, without denying the differences among them, can and should make an effort to live together peacefully amid their disagreements and disparate priorities.

[The following are the ten principles, excerpted from their supporting narrative, and provided here with the kind permission of the authors and the Zondervan Publishing House.]

1. Thou shalt acknowledge thine own finite and sinful nature and, thus, the limited scope of thy perspective.
2. Thou shalt acknowledge thy brother or sister may disagree with thee and yet remain deserving of thy respect as a brother or sister.
3. Thou shalt learn to articulate fairly, honestly, and thoroughly the positions of thy opponent.
4. Thou shalt follow the path toward truth even when it challenges thy previous conclusions and beliefs.

5. Thou shalt encourage independent thinking rather than conformity, seeking to educate before seeking to persuade.
6. Thou shalt seek to understand and to acknowledge how thine own presuppositions, biases, and personal experiences may influence thy perspectives on various issues.
7. Thou shalt resist the temptation to stereotype and shalt instead realize that generalities often mask important distinctions.
8. Thou shalt recognize, in this pluralistic nation, the important difference between shaping public policy based on Christian values and instituting public policy that is specifically Christian.
9. Thou shalt make a special effort to consider the viewpoints of those who, based on educational specialty or personal proximity, may have greater insight or a more informed perspective than the average citizen.
10. Thou shalt, when in doubt, risk erring on the side of the most vulnerable.

Selected Bibliography

Black, Charles L. *A New Birth of Freedom: Human Rights, Named and Unnamed.* New York: Grosset-Putnam, 1997. [IP, AM]

Boston, Robert. *Why the Religious Right Is Wrong about Separation of Church and State.* Buffalo NY: Prometheus Books, 1993. [IP, ERBS]

Carter, Stephen. *The Culture of Disbelief: How American Law and Politics Trivialize Religious Devotion.* New York: Basic Books, 1993. [IP, ERBS]

Davis, Derek. *Original Intent: Chief Justice Rehnquist and the Course of American Church/State Relations.* Buffalo NY: Prometheus Books, 1991. [IP, AM, OSV]

Eastland, Terry, ed. *Religious Liberty in the Supreme Court: The Cases That Defined the Debate over Church and State.* Washington DC: Ethics and Public Policy Center./Grand Rapids: Eerdmans, 1993. [IP]

Estep, William. *The Revolution Within the Revolution: The First Amendment in Historical Context, 1612-1789.* Grand Rapids: Eerdmans, 1990.

Frame, Randall L., and Tharpe, Alan. *How Right Is the Right?: A Biblical and Balanced Approach to Politics.* Grand Rapids: Zondervan, 1996. [IP]

Galston, William A. *Liberal Purposes: Goods, Virtues, and Diversity in the Liberal State.* Cambridge: Cambridge University Press, 1991. [IP, AM]

Hinson, E. Glenn. *Religious Liberty: The Christian Roots of Our Fundamental Freedoms.* Louisville KY: Glad River Publications, 1991. [IP]

Hunter, James Davison. *Culture Wars: The Struggle To Define America.* New York: Basic Books, 1991. [IP, ERBS]

Hunter, James Davison, and OS Guinness, eds. *Articles of Faith, Articles of Peace: The Religious Liberty Clauses and the American Public Philosophy.* Washington DC: Brookings Institution, 1990. [IP, ERBS]

Jaffa, Henry V. *Original Intent and the Frames of the Constitution: A Disputed Question.* Washington DC: Regnery Gateway, 1994. [IP, AM]

Kirk, Russell. *The Roots of American Order.* 3rd ed. Washington DC: Regnery Gateway, 1991. [IP, AM]

Kramnick, Isaac, and Moore, R. Laurence. *The Godless Constitution: The Case Against Religious Correctness.* New York: W. W. Norton, 1996. [IP, ERBS]

Levy, Leonard W. *Original Intent and the Framer's Constitution.* New York: Macmillan, 1988. [IP, OSV]

_____. *The Establishment Clause: Religion and the First Amendment.* 2d ed. New York: Macmillan, 1986. [IP, ERBS]

Macedo, Steven. *Liberal Virtues: Citizenship, Virtue, and Community in Liberal Constitutionalism.* Oxford: Clarendon Press, 1990. [IP, AM]

Madison, James. *Notes of Debates in the Federal Convention of 1787*. New York: W. W. Norton, 1987. [IP]

Miller, Robert T., and Flowers, Ronald B. *Toward Benevolent Neutrality: Church, State, and the Supreme Court*. 4th ed. Waco TX: Baylor University Press, 1992. [IP, OSV]

Neuhaus, Richard John. *The Naked Public Square*. 2d ed. Grand Rapids: Eerdmans, 1984. [IP, ERBS]

Noll, Mark A., Nathan O. Hatch, and George M. Marsden, *The Search for Christian America*. Westchester IL: Crossway Books, 1983. [IP, ERBS]

Nord, Warren A. *Religion and American Education: Rethinking a National Dilemma*. Chapel Hill NC: University of North Carolina Press, 1995. [IP, AM]

Novak, Michael. *Free Persons and the Common Good*. Lanham MD: Madison Books, 1989. [IP, OSV]

Pfeffer, Leo. *Church, State, and Freedom*. Rev. Ed. Boston: Beacon Press, 1967. [AM]

_____. *Religion, State, and the Burger Court*. Buffalo NY: Prometheus Books, 1984. [IP, AM]

Rakove, Jack N. *Original Meanings: Politics and Ideas in the Making of the Constitution*. New York: Random House/Vintage Books, 1997. [IP, OSV]

Sandel, Michael. *Democracy's Discontents: America in Search of a Public Philosophy*. Cambridge MA: Harvard University/Belknap Press, 1996. [IP, OSV]

Smith, Gary Scott. *God and Politics—Four Views on the Reformation of Civil Government: Theonomy, Principled Pluralism, Christian America, National Confessionalism*. Phillipsburg NJ: Presbyterian and Reformed, 1989. [IP]

Sowell, Thomas. *A Conflict of Visions: The Ideological Origins of Political Struggles*. New York: William Morrow and Company/Quill, 1987. [IP, OSV]

Wood, James E., ed. *The First Freedom: Religion and the Bill of Rights*. Waco TX: Dawson Institute, Baylor University, 1990. [IP]

Key
[AM] = Advanced Material
[ERBS] = Especially Recommended for Beginning Study
[IP] = In Print [OSV] = Of Special Value